SEGUNDA EDICION

© by EDITORIAL EVEREST, S. A. · LEON
Carretera León-La Coruña, km 5 - LEON (Spain)
All rights reserved
ISBN: 84-241-4622-0
Legal deposit: 1270-1984
The total or partial reproduction
of this book is forbidden
Printed in Spain

EDITORIAL EVERGRAFICAS, S. A.
Carretera León-La Coruña, km 5
LEON (Spain)

GRAN CANARIA
LANZAROTE
FUERTEVENTURA

Text: MANUEL GONZÁLEZ SOSA

Photographs: CIGANOVIC with the colaboration
of Salmer and Edistudio
Juan M. Ruiz
Molina

AL MERITO TURISTICO

MINISTERIO DE INFORMACION
Y TURISMO — ESPAÑA

EDITORIAL EVEREST, S. A.

MADRID • LEON • BARCELONA • SEVILLA • GRANADA • VALENCIA
ZARAGOZA • BILBAO • LAS PALMAS DE GRAN CANARIA • LA CORUÑA
PALMA DE MALLORCA • ALICANTE — MEXICO • BUENOS AIRES

IN THE BEGINNING THERE WAS THE FABLE

Before being discovered and even before being a predicted reality, the Canary Islands were a creation of the imagination of man, who, to fulfill his nostalgia for Paradise, dreamed up a land of delights in the middle of the terrible ocean. This is where we get the name Fortunate Islands as they were known in times long ago. Then, when the pioneers of Atlantic navigation dared turn their backs on the Pillars of Hercules, these rocks were glimpsed and touched, perhaps by accident, and then the collective memory of classic antiquity, and even the writings of the most famous ancient authors (Homer, Plato, Plutarch, etc), picked up the fabulous echoes of the secrets divulged by those who ventured furthest out onto the Dark Sea. These echoes, more or less altered were later repeated by the Arab writers only to be completely silenced in the Middle Ages, when, as is known, the ocean and the imagination of the people were again filled not with information and glimpses of the truth but with fantastic creatures and happenings. When the fog of the Middle Ages lifted, the Canary Archipelago was again discovered and correct information and familiarity with the courses of the Atlantic forcefully awoke the greed of the adventurers who fell on these lands like birds of prey. This was the time when, after the rule of the Genoese pirate, Lancelotto Malocello, there were expeditions of pirates and merchants from the Mediterranean (Florence, Genoa, Majorca, Catalunia, Andalucia) who put into the island not in scarch of ideals, but mainly to get all they could out of the mine of slaves which was what the native population signified to them. The first attempts at exploitation were carried out entirely at the risk of the instigators, without the leadership or guidance of any prince or state. With the first Portuguese and Castilian attempts (1393), there is a change in the relationship between the people of Europe and the Canary Islands. Especially with Juan de Bethencourt, a Norman knight in the service of Enrique III of Castile, the purposes of the conquest and colonization acquired the characteristics of a political endeavour; this endeavour, when reverted, after many vicissitudes, to the Crown of the Catholic Kings, in 1477, became enriched by the important project, based on the conversion and civilization of the inhabitants, which was embarked on by these rulers. In 1496, with the conquest of the last of the islands, Tenerife (Gran Canaria had been incorporated into Castile in 1483), the Canary Archipelago began to make its mark on the History of Spain. From that time on, it has formed an integral part of History, sharing together with the other parts of the national territory, in the unity of the nation's destiny. All this was done without indering the islands' own individual biography, which has not been exactly idyllic and obscure, but rather more agonizing and notorious due to its location at an important intersection on the planet.

«The finger of God» in the Port of Las Nieves. ▶

The Canary Islands in the «Atlas catalán de 1375», probably the work of Cresques Abraham and Jafudá Cresques.

Las Palmas. Balcony of *Columbus's House* with the arms of Don Fernando Guanarteme.

THE ARCHIPELAGO

The Canary Archipelago is located in the Atlantic Ocean, facing the coast of the Sahara Desert (Africa), between the North latitudes 27° and 29°, therefore very near the Tropic of Cancer and a little to the East of the zero meridian. Its geological origin has long been a subject for discussion and it continues to awaken the interest of investigators. From among the various theories proposed in relation to this matter, we should mention, as an example of antipodal solutions, in conception and chronology, the one which takes the islands to be ostensible vestiges of the Atlantis, that fabulous submerged continent (the hypothesis is scientifically unfounded and has, therefore, been discarded), and the one which believes that the islands slowly immerged from the bottom of the sea as a result of successive volcanic eruptions. As the lava accumulated at the edge of the abysmal craters, these eruptions ended up by spreading out over the surface of the ocean the various layers that form the basis of the island group.

Presumably, around the year 3000 B.C. the first inhabitants landed on the islands, these were the «guanches», large men with white skin, blue eyes and blond hair, who constituted the basis of the native population which Castile finally subdued in the XVI century. These men belonged to the Mechtael-Arbi race which foreshadowed, in a very advanced phase, the Cromagnon race and which has been detected primarily in Algeria. What is known of their customs and practices denotes a rather advanced stage of moral evolution which did not, however, correspond to their backward technical level. We can get an idea of the importance of the instrumental poverty of the guanches (due to their almost complete isolation) from the fact that they completely forgot how to navigate a thing which their forefathers were undoubtedly familiar with although on a very rudimentary level, when they came to the islands. With regard to their language, it is very probable that, as well as other elements of their civilization, it was a contribution of a Semitic type Mediterranean race which later, in prehistoric times, mixed in with the original «guanche» people.

The present population of the Canary Islands is the result of the fusion of the native race with the Spanish conquerors, colonials and later immigrants, who were responsible for the fundamental contributions; and also, although to a lesser degree, with other European elements which for one reason or another, established themselves in the archipelago over the centuries. Politically speaking, the territory of the Canary Islands consists of two provinces of the Spanish nation, forming, from the moment of its incorporation into the Crown of Spain, an integral part of the metropolitan entity, on a completely equal level with the other peninsular regions.

Cauldron of the Pines at Gáldar. ▶

Gáldar. Caves of the *guanches*.

The heraldic dogs of Gran Canaria, in the Plaza de Santa Ana in Las Palmas.

GRAN CANARIA

The Canary Archipelago is formed by seven islands and six small barren islands divided into two groups: The Western group formed by the islands of Tenerife, La Gomera, El Hierro and La Palma (the administrative area of the province of Santa Cruz de Tenerife), and the Eastern Group, or Province of Las Palmas —the topic of this book— composed of the islands of Gran Canaria, Lanzarote and Fuerteventura, and the smaller ones known as La Graciosa, Alegranza, Isla de Lobos, Roque del Este, Roque del Oeste and Montaña Clara, the first of which is the only one inhabited.

The island of Gran Canaria consists of a rocky mass of volcanic origin rising up to nearly 2,000 meters above sea level in the form of a cone-shaped pyramid. The most outstanding characteristics of its relief are determined by the large ravines radiating from the center peaks out towards the four points of the compass. Geologically, it is divided into two large well differentiated counties: the «new island», extends to the Northwest and includes the most fertile and inhabited zones; and the «old island», located to the Southwest, where the dominant feature is the planetary skeleton worn away by erosion. The landscape of the latter presents, within its dramatic modulation, a certain monotony, especially when we remember the multiplicity of aspects offered by the other half. The «new island» has come to be like a small country that summarizes all the landscapes of the land and that even, daring to attempt more, gives us an idea of the lunar landscape. This kaleidoscopic show is even more surprising when we stop to remember how small the island area really is —1,532 square kilometers— and contributing factors not only include geology and relief, but also, to a great extent, the plant life and the climate. We must point out that the climate is not uniform although always within the framework of mild conditions in general, there are a series of variations, simultaneously determined by the altitude and the situation of the land. The coastal outline also falls under this heading of diversity. The Northwest coast from Tinocas onwards is steep and rocky, unapproachable in parts and, in others, dotted with coves and inlets and an occasional beach with greyish sand or gravel; at the same time, the Southern coast, which includes a large part of the island outline, almost completely unfolds in a succession of golden beaches of varying sizes, ending up in the great sandy plain of the delta of Maspalomas, which is the southern-most point of the island.

The population of Gran Canaria has now reached 520,000 inhabitants, of which 275,000 live in the capital, Las Palmas.

Canary Island girl. ▶

The sheer west coast contrasts with the dunes of Maspalomas in the south.

LAS PALMAS

LAS PALMAS DE GRAN CANARIA is a city full of attractions. These attractions range from the natural scene —the warm bright atmosphere, golden beaches, colorful plant life— to the everyday spectacle of cosmopolitan humanity to be seen in the streets and in squares; from the cordiality of its people to the delight of the climate; from the picturesque and tempting world of its international commerce —Hindus, Jews, Lebanese, Moroccans, etc.— to the folklore and the local sports; from the manifestations of its important cultural life to the very complete network of installations for amusement and relaxation which has set off an enterprising tourist industry...

It was founded in 1478 by the Spanish conqueror Juan Rejón, and is located in the Northeastern part of Gran Canaria, under the shadow of the «tombolo» or appendix of lava, which at this point abruptly breaks up the *almost* circular circumference outlining the island. This peninsular addition is called La Isleta, and the narrow strip, once submerged, which connects it to the main part of the island is called the Isthmus of Guanarteme. Until a few years ago, the city occupied only a strip of coraline formation dating back to the Fourth Period; but, at present, it also includes large areas taken from the sea, as well as the hill sides and the group of hills that once served as its backdrop. From the distant sector of San Cristóbal, located to the South, to La Isleta, which is the northern point, the urban frame extends approximately nine kilometers, in a succession of sectors that are differentiated by their special architectural physiognomy and even, in a certain way, by the distinct ways of life of the majority of the inhabitants in each neighborhood. These sectors listed from South to North, are as follows: the already mentioned *San Cristóbal* (until not long ago, a population exclusively of fishermen); *Vegueta* (which constitutes the survival of the original city); *Los Arenales* which is really the conglomeration of four dissimilar neighborhoods (Los Arenales is actually Lugo, Ciudad Jardin and Las Alcaravaneras); *Refugio* and *La Isleta*. These last two form the large, diverse section commonly known as *Puerto de la Luz*. The following are the non-coastal sectors, from North to South, along a rather zig-zag line: *Guanarteme; Escaleritas; Schamann; San Antonio;* the *Peaks* of *San Lázaro, San Nicolás, San Francisco, San Roque* and *San Juan* and finally, *San José* astride between some uncultivated hills and the once luxurious Valley of San José, located between San Cristóbal and Vegueta; *Las Rehoyas* and *Lomo Apolinario* are somewhat marginal although directly attached to the population, and are the very recent consequences of the strong demographic growth of Las Palmas.

Partial view of Las Palmas.

VEGUETA, GENIUS AND FORM

VEGUETA is the main sector of Las Palmas. It was originally a military camp: the «Real de las Palmas», set up, crudely and provisionally, on June 24, 1478, by the Spanish conquerors who arrived that day on Gran Canaria under the command of captain Juan Rejón. The spot chosen was a grove of palm trees, on the right bank of the Guiniguada gorge, a few yards from its outlet and these palm trees are the name and the emblem of Las Palmas. «Segura tiene La Palma». Then, once the conquest of the island was over, the area around this stronghold began to be transformed into an urban nucleus more or less hazardously designed which soon became the seat and centre of the Spanish monarchy's political, military and ecclesiastic activities in their incipient colonization of the Atlantic. The material reflection of these intial and subsequent stages can still be glimpsed in the physiognomy of Vegueta, which constitutes perhaps the most interesting architectural group bequeathed by the past centuries to the Canary archipelago. Here we find a variety of examples of the most diverse styles and especially of the flowery Gothic style, to be seen in façades and patios, graceful, early overseas modulations. Its spiritual atmosphere also seems filled with whispers of olden days. For this reason, the observant traveller, whose imagination is sensitive to historical and traditional suggestions, will discover many moving experiences. He will be able to contemplate streets and houses that suggest colonial architecture; wide balconies with lattice work, small hidden plazas; corners and alleys; shaded entrances through which you can catch a glimpse here and there of the bright flowering, intimacy of a patio... And all this is preserved and cared for with a sensitivity which has known how to combine the respect for the past, in all its most valuable aspects, with intelligent fidelity to the spirit of our times.

Vegueta contains the Cathedral, which was built between the second half of the XVI century and the end of the XIX; the Episcopal Palace, which is somber but charming; the hermitage of San Antonio Abad, built over the foundation of a primitive chapel, where Christopher Columbus must have attended mass during the course of his journey which ended in the Discovery; the Consistorial Houses, in Neoclassic style; the church of Santo Domingo; the little plaza of the Espíritu Santo, with its delightful covered fountain («so that the water will not get wet»); plaza de Santa Ana...

In this part of the city we also find the Canary Island Museum (Anthropology) and the House of Columbus, which constitutes a cultural complex consisting of the Columbus Museum, the Provincial Museum of Fine Arts and the Provincial Historical Archives.

We also have here the monument in the old cemetery erected in memory of the poet Tomás Morales, which is an admirable work by the great Spanish sculptor Victorio Macho.

Facade of St. Anne's Cathedral in Las Palmas. ▶

Interior of the cathedral.

«Dolorosa», by the Canary Island sculptor José Luján Pérez (c. XVIII), in
the cathedral.

Chapel of St. Anthony the
Abbot.

Facade of the Town Hall of Las Palmas.

The tranquil Plaza de Santo Domingo.

The little square of the Holy Spirit, with its neoclassical
fountain.

CULTURAL AND ARTISTIC LIFE

The varied and relatively intense cultural activity of Las Palmas is a phenomenum which should be mentioned. With regard to the fine arts, we should point out the «Luján Pérez» School. Famous because of the pedagogic ideals which inspired its foundation fifty years ago based on the principle of respecting the creative personality of its pupils. The city also has various exhibition rooms and two important museums: the Provincial Museum of Fine Arts, with an annex of the monographic room dedicated to the island painter Nicolás Massieu, and the Néstor Museum containing a large collection of the works of the famous painter Néstor Martín Fernández de la Torre. (The Antonio Padrón Museum is at present installed in Gáldar a town inland). In Las Palmas we also find several Municipal Accademies of Painting, Sculpture and Ceramics. In the theater field, we must point out, within the framework of experimental theater, the Teatro Insular de Camara and the Teatro de Arte de Las Palmas, amongst others. With regard to music, there is the Royal Philharmonic Society and its Orchestra; in addition, apart from the activities of several private chamber music groups, there is the work done by the Juventudes Musicales and the Canary Island Group of Friends of the Opera. Here, literary activity is especially intense, in the area of creation as well as in that of publishing. Research and accademic life not only on the institutional level, belong to the Canary Museum, the Society of Medical Science, the Canary Institute of Regional Medicine, the Institute of Economic Studies, and other centers. Las Palmas is also the headquarters of the International University of the Canary Islands, particularly dedicated to the holding of courses on Spanish culture for foreigners; but it is also involved in humanistic and scientific teachings of a general nature, with conferences two or three times a year. We must mention the Canary Museum as such because it contains important ethnographic and anthropologic collections dedicated to the primitive inhabitants of the archipelago. These collections include tools, arms, ceramics, etc., with the especially interesting and notable collection of bone remains. Also interesting is the cultural complex of the House of Columbus which consists of the Columbus Museum, dedicated to the records of the Discoverer's visits to Gran Canaria, and of the Provincial Museum of Fine Arts the House of the Hidalgo and the Provincial Historical Archive containing in the same way as the library and the archives of the Canary Museum, valuable documents on the history of these islands. The Pérez Galdós House Museum preserves manuscripts and personal articles belonging to the great novelist, a native of Las Palmas. The recently installed Provincial Public Library is a model for all others of its kind.

◀ Carpet of flowers in a Las Palmas street, during the festival of Corpus Christi.

Facade of the Provincial Museum of Fine Arts.

One of the facades of the House-Museum of
Columbus.

Renaissance courtyard in the House-Museum of
Columbus.

A room in the House-Museum of Columbus.

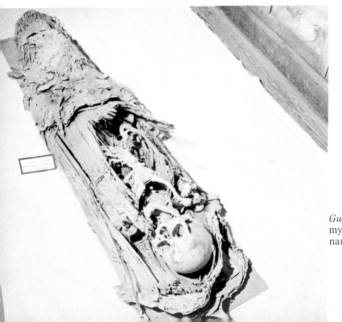

Guanche mummy in the Canary Museum.

Various types of *guanche* pottery in the Canary Museum.

Bust of Christopher Columbus in the avenue of his name.

TRIANA AND LOS ARENALES

Triana, is chronologically speaking, the first important shoot of the urban expansion of Las Palmas. It sprang up on the left bank of the Guiniguada during the times following the cristalization of the old city (Vegueta). It was named by immigrants from Andalusia due to certain topographic similarities to the sector of the same name in Seville. It was then, and still is now, a predominately commercial district. It preserves the old names of the streets as reminders of European merchants, who played a big role here. Although this part of the city is noted more for its outlook towards the future than for its reverence to the past it is still possible to find corners and buildings which recall the discreet elegance of the past. Let us mention for example the church of San Francisco and the hermitage of San Telmo, in an elegant architectural style, with its outstanding Moorish-Christian panelling and some lovely images, including an Inmaculada, which is apparently bi Alonso Cano. The Alameda de Colón, Plazuela de Hurtado de Mendoza, San Telmo Park, the plaza of Cairasco, in front of the Gabinete Literario (Literary Cabinet) constitute four pleasant parentheses right in the middle of the bustling trade and commerce of the city.

In the same way as Los Arenales (which is in fact a direct extension), Triana contains several important centres and public organisms, such as the civil government, Military government, Finance Delegation, General captaincy of the Canary Island Naval Base and Council offices. But, above all, Triana is an extremely important commercial centre. In this aspect, we have the main street, called Calle Mayor de Triana, which is the headquarters for many different establishments where the most varied products from

Europe North America and Asia are sold, all of which has been made possible by the fact that Las Palmas is a free port area. The exotic tone here is a result of the Hindu bazar, with their well stocked, tempting showcases, and the rather less glittering shops belonging to people from Asia: Syrians, Jordanians, Lebanese, etc.

Within the area of Los Arenales, we must mention the Provincial Public Library and the large educational complex formed by the two High School Institutes, the Initiation Center, for Higher Education (Engineering and Architecture) Teachars college, School of Technical Engineers and the School of Commerce.

A corner of the Plaza de San Francisco.

◀ «El Gabinete Literario», in the little square of
Cairasco.

San Telmo Park.

...terior of the Pérez Galdós Theatre.

CIUDAD JARDÍN, LAS ALCARAVANERAS

Between Los Arenales and the district of Puerto de la Luz we find a large sector which is formed principally by the Ciudad Jardín, Las Alcaravaneras and the expansion area facing the neighborhood of Guanarteme. All these centers present different physionomies although they find a common denominator in the fact that they are more or less modern in relation to the sectors described until now. The Ciudad Jardín is a beautifully urbanized residential district, with some of the most attractive corners of the modern city. For example, we have the Doramas Park which is outstanding not because of its size, as it is quite small, but because of the quality and rarity of the vegetation which includes some very beautiful examples of Canary plant life. Other atractions of the park are its swimming pools and its interesting zoo. The Doramas Park, also contains the Hotel Santa Catalina, and, on the crest of the hill up to where the so-called «Jardines Rubio» extend, there is a night club called Altavista, with its terraces providing one of the most suggestive panoramic views of Las Palmas. On one side of this park, forming a part of it, there is the Pueblo Canario. This is a very lovely architectural group dedicated to the exhibition of interesting elements of folklore (crafts dances, etc). It was built according to the plans of Néstor Martín Fernández de la Torre *(Néstor)*, for the purpose of giving it artistic qualities superior to the popular architecture of the Islands. This explains the fact that the Néstor Museum is located here, housing numerous canvases and drawings (including the «Poema del Mar» and the «Poema de la Tierra»), as well as rare or valuable objects and the personal belongings from his studio.

The m st outstanding feature of Las Alcaravaneras is its splendid beach of the same name, situated facing Puerto de la Luz. Running alongside, but on a higher leveb, there is a wide avenue planted with palm trees, from where there is a lovely view out over the bay and beach itself. At its northernmost end, there is the Nautical Club, with its magnificent modern building and excellent installations. The Insular Stadium is also situated in Las Alcaravaneras and is used for national football matches.

Between Las Alcaravaneras and the sector of Guanarteme with the plaza de la Victoria as its center, an urban nucleus has recently grown up which stands out because of the width of its streets and the audacity of the architectural design of the buildings, which is dictated by a desire to move upwards, otherwise unknown in the city. Nearby, we have the Central Market, the Arsenal of the Canary Islands Naval Base and the Casa del Marino (Sailor's House) which is an institution of international importance.

The «Rubió Gardens» and the Santa Catalina hotel, in the Doramas Park.

FOLKLORE

Canary Island folklore, taken in its widest sense, offers a great wealth of expressions. Dancing, singing, ceramics, games, magic, practiques, etc., supply sufficient material for an extensive exposition even when summarized. A commom characteristic of all these folklorical expressions is their clear hispanic lineage, although in some cases enriched by the contributions from other regions, especially from Portugal and Spanish America. The faint inheritance from the native race can also be traced in a few areas.

DANCES AND SONGS. Outstanding among such popular creations are the songs and dances which depict the spiritual elegance of the Canary Islanders and their peaceful and affectionate nature, as well as their fine sense of humor.

«Folías», «Isas», «Malagueñas», «Seguidillas»... Here are some of the dances and songs of the Canary Island people, which are accompanied by several instruments, always including the guitar and the «timple». This instrument boils down to a very small guitar with five string, making a bold, sharp and rapid sound, giving the popular Canary music special character. The «folía» —dance, ballad and melody— is the most important lyrical expression of the collective spirit of the Canary Island. The «isa» —dance and song— is a very unique Atlantic version of the «jota»: a «jota» which is light in tension, less vibrant, more polished and very pleasant. As its name indicates, the «malagueña» has been derived from the Andalusian song of the same name. In this rapid, and very incomplete list we must not leave out the «arroro»: the outstanding lullaby of the Islanders; this song, sung with feeling by the Island women, is converted into a moving expression of motherly love.

CRAFTS. Here, as everywhere else, there are traditional activities which produce articles which are outstanding because their perfect combination of the utilitariau and the aesthetic. Of all these crafts, we must point out the famous Island embroidery and drawn thread work, which are very lovely. We could say about the same, although on a less refined scale, about the basketweaving, using palm leaves, cane and reeds as materials for the creations.

The ceramic work is another of the artisan activities which is well established in the Archipelago. In a certain way, this is a trade inherited directly from the native population, whose technique and models are repeated, although with evident impoverishment, by the Canary potter of today. He, just like his cave men ascendants, continues to ignore the existence, in this day and age, of the potter's wheel; and the jars which they make with their hands and which are still used in the rural areas, assume the shapes originally formed in prehistoric times. This is the secret of the special charm of these jars and pots which combine elegance and roughness in a strange synthesis.

◀ Popular dances and songs in the *Pueblo Canario*. ▶

THE PUERTO DE LA LUZ

The houses of the Puerto de la Luz, as an urban district of Las Palmas, occupy a large area and the district is formed by several sectors of a different nature although these have the one common vibrating feature supplied by the bustling port activity. It extends from the border of Las Alcaravaneras to the shore and the southern hillsides of La Isleta, and it of course includes the isthmus connecting the latter to the island itself. This whole part of the city is a direct result of the vitality of the Puerto de la Luz. This port unites really exceptional natural conditions which predicted, from the very beginning, the outstanding role it plays today in the panorama of the great world ports. This one piece of information is sufficient to give us an idea of its present importance: in relation to the movement of ships and the amount of gross tonnages handled, the Puerto de la Luz boasts as being the first in Spain and third in the world. Its strategic location on the European-American and European-African routes, together with its excellent natural and man-made conditions, have converted it into an exceptional supply station for the large ships which weave an intricate network of intercontinental voyages over the Atlantic. These voyages do not only affect Gran Canaria in a tangential way, but they also begin or end here as a result of the heavy maritime traffic produced by the tourist currents and especially by the intense international commerce developed on the island. In addition to this, we must point out that it is a great fishing port, also occupiying first place among those of Spain. Its nearness to the Canary-Sahara shoals and all its insurpassable conditions, as well as excellent supply facilities, are the reasons it has been chosen as a stop-over and provision post by some of the most important fishing fleets of the world, including the Japanese one, which has made this its permanent base for activity in this part of the Atlantic. A logical result of this plural importance is the technical level of the equipment and installations of the Puerto de la Luz, which are maintained constantly up-to —date, using everything that contributes to the maximum efficiency of harbor activities—. Such care also extends to cleanliness and order on the docks and walks, to such a degree that we can say that this is perhaps one of the cleanest ports on our Planet; an added feature is the fragrance and lovely color of the flowers in the numerous gardens.

The most important comercial streets of the Puerto de la Luz are the Albareda, Ferreras, la Naval and, above all, Juan Rejón. The latter contains the majority of the Indian bazars which are so famous and so tempting.

Partial view of the port. ▶

The Port of
La Luz: one
of the most
important in
the world.

The old Castle of La Luz.

Santa Catalina Park, centre of cosmopolitan Las Palmas.

SANTA CATALINA PARK

One of the main elements of animation and cosmopolitan commerce offered daily in the Puerto de la Luz is, without a doubt, the variety of people continually making their way through its streets, plazas and docks, creating, with their presence, an atmosphere suggesting a world market place, an acumenical square, just like in the great maritime or land cross-roads on the most important, routes of the world. For this reason, a walk through the port area has come to be something like reviewing all the races of the world, like looking at a very rich, colorful «costumbrista» series of historical pictures; or, too, listening with enjoyment to the sound —soft, or harsh or singing but always fascinating— of almost all the languages of our Planet; we have a warm feeling of universal fraternity which begins to take hold of us as the apparent and picturesque things give way to the evidence of the essential identity of mankind.

This bustling and in a large part exotic world acts and moves throughout the city, but this occurs especially in the port area, preferably in a place which for this reason has been converted into perhaps the most attractive spot in Las Palmas.

We are referring to the Santa Catalina Park located at the beginning of the dock of the same name, not far from Las Canteras beach. This is quite a small park, but it is not lacking in vegetation; here there is an abundance of stands full of magazines and a large range of the most sur-prising and tempting articles. From dawn until the late hours of the night, especially from October to April, this park offers an animated and multi-colored view of human life supplied, by the color and diversity of the throngs of people. Scandinavian tourists, gesturing Italian sailors. Ja-panese or Korean fishermen, inhabitants from the nearby Sahara. colored people from Mauritania, Sierra Leone, Monrovia, Senegal; Hindu women with their «saris» of floating, subtle beauty, foreign wandering painters exhibiting their works and the spectacle of their artistic skill in the open air... All in all, a lively showcase of races and nations, whose renewed presence constitutes one of the most interesting attractions of the city of Las Palmas. Their presence has taught the city's inhabitants the art of cordiality and understanding and this custom is certainly one of the most interesting and most positive characteristics of their personality. This cordiality is always active and consistent, ruled at all times by an exquisite tact that keeps them from, falling as sometimes happens in other places, into excesses which could mean a disrespectful attack on intimacy or foreign convictions; and this occurs of course, without hampering the islander's own concept of life and things.

A view of the city, with Santa Catalina Park in the foreground. ▶

LAS CANTERAS BEACH

Without a doubt one of the greatest attractions of Las Palmas, as a tourist area, is the beach of Las Canteras. This is situated within the city limits, in the large bay of Confital, behind the inner harbor of the Puerto de la Luz, along the coastal curve that is formed on the Northwestern strip of the isthmus or «gollete», where La Isleta is connected to the island. It is approximately four kilometers long and it unfolds in a succession of large and comfortable areas covered with extremely fine, golden sand. In addition to its other excellent conditions considered here normal, Las Canteras offers the advantages derived from its famous «barra» which is a kind of natural breakwater of madreporic formation that runs from end to end about two hundred meters from the shore, in the form of a gang plank separating the coastal waters from the open sea, thus protecting the beach from the Atlantic waves that break against the wall. A long walk without a railing runs from end to end, hugging the curves of the coast serving as an approach and an observation point for the beach. Here, we can also swim at night because of the splendid lighting which has been provided for the beach. Along this walk and in the streets and plazas nearby, we find hotels, residences, apartments restaurants, night-clubs and all other types of establishments ideal for enjoying one's leisure to the utmost. This walk as well as the wide space between the plaza de Manuel Becerra, right at the entrance to the Muelle Grande (Dock) on La Isleta, and calle Churruca, in the Guanarteme sector, and from the Dock of Santa Catalina to the street Portugal, constitute the setting for the animated and intense night life of Las Palmas.

But Las Canteras is, above all, the solarium of the people from the Northern part of Europe, who literally flock to this sunny beach at the first sign of cold weather in their own country. The reason is that, in spite of its relative nearness to the Old Continent, here in the winter the people can enjoy the delights of a warm, sunny climate.

There are other aspects of the landscape that surround Las Canteras and contribute to its reputation as a unique and delightful spot. On one side, there are the mountains of the island that climb upward in a succession of different and changing colors, moving toward the central peaks; and on the other side, there are the red lava of La Isleta and the old fishing neighborhood of La Puntilla, with its smell of saltpeter and its lively picturesqueness. And at the back, at the end of the outline of Gran Canaria, there is the Mountain of Galdar, like a copy of the Peak of Tenerife, the famous Teide, whose silhouette rises majestically up into the sky, almost in the very center of the distant horizon.

The popular beach of Las Canteras.

Aspects of Las
Canteras beach.

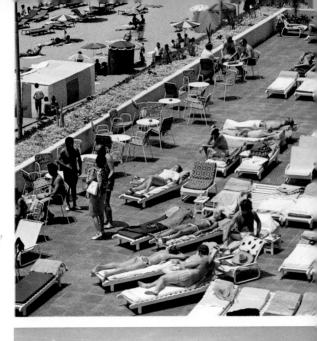

Promenade of Las Canteras beach.

THE POPULAR SECTORS AND THE HIGH CITY

THE POPULAR SECTORS. Those with the most distinct personality are the following: La Isleta, Guanartema, Los Riscos, San José and San Cristóbal.

Facing the bay of the Puerto de la Luz and seated on the southern side of the promontory that forms La Isleta, the sector of the same name contributes to the human and urban landscape of Las Palmas with very singular characteristics. It is a large and heavily populated area, with wide streets in some stretches, and in other parts with labyrinthine curves such as in La Puntilla, the home of «bajura» fishermen. As we might imagine, La Isleta is the lively setting of many types of people (stable and transitory) who are more or less directly involved in the trade and the adventures of the sea, in all its facets.

Guanartema is another great port sector. It begins almost at the Santa Catalina Park just where the street Fernando Guanarteme (the name of the last native king) starts, and has come to be, in a large part, influenced by the beach of Las Canteras, especially by the section called «playa chica». This explains why a large proportion of the best tourist installations of Las Palmas are to be found here.

At the other end of the city, or in other words, within the area of traditional Las Palmas (where we find Vegueta and Triana), there are Los Riscos, the most popular neighborhoods which are, without a doubt, the source of the picturesque mythology of the «sainetes» or farces and the island picaresque literature. These «Riscos» or peaks occupy the slopes and tops of the hills which serve as the background for Vegueta and, especially for Triana; we at once notice the houses here, not so much because of the anarchical form of arrangement but more because of the lively, diverse colors of their façades. There are five «Riscos»: Risco de San Juan, Risco de San Roque, Risco de San Nicolás, Risco de San Francisco and Risco de San Lázaro.

San José is also a heavily populated and lively neighborhood San Cristóbal, a place with a great fishing tradition and juicy legends, is now coming to the end of days, as it is to be absorbed by a vast residential and recreational urbanization.

THE HIGH CITY. This name has been given to the group of satellite towns which have recently sprung up on several of the hills that serve as the backdrop for the districts of Los Arenales, Ciudad Jardín and Las Alcaravaneras. These are large centers, predominately filled with wide-open spaces and views of the sea, which can be seen from one side to the other, and numerous green parks and sports installations. These centers are: Schamann Escaleritas and Buenavista. Here we must take special note of the great Avenue of Escaleritas, where we find the highest buildings in the city, and of the Paseo de la Cornisa, which is a great look-out point over the low part of the city, the port and its horizon.

A modern church in the Ciudad Alta.

Monument to León y Castillo.

A modern building in the Plaza de Don Benito.

SPORTS

All the sports universally practised, with the exception of those which need snow, have become established here, especially in the capital. Of course, soccer brags of holding first place and this sport is favored by the excellent natural conditions of the islands. In addition to others that are less perfect and scattered throughout the capital and province, Las Palmas has a very adequate stadium in which its team regularly competes with the others in the First National Division. Swimming is another activity in which the sons of the Archipelago have excelled on an international level. With regard to golf, in Gran Canaria there are such important and renowned courses as the Golf Club —the oldest in Spain— combining its superb installations and comfortable conditions with the fact that it is located in an exceptionally beautiful spot: on the edge of the volcanic crater of Bandama; and the course of the tourist complex at Maspalomas, in the southern part of the island, next to the large beach of the same name. Tennis, basketball, judo, bicycling, automobile racing, etc., can be enjoyed easily by participating or merely as a spectator. Equestrian and mountain sports are activities that are perhaps still in the beginning stages of development. Hunting and fishing fans (especially the latter) are able to find here numerous places and opportunities for these activities. Partridges, rabbits, ducks, wild pigeons, gulls and other small game species can be found on Gran Canaria as well as on the other islands, especially Lanzarote and Fuerteventura. Since this country is dominated by the ocean, it is natural that nautical sports are practised in all their varieties, with the additional feature that they can be enjoyed from January to January because of the mild climate. Here we must take special note, since it is one of the typical local sporting events, of the so called regattas of «botes», which involve boats with a large latin sail which is quite out of proportion in comparison with the frame. These regattas always bring out crowds of people who throng along the shore. keeping up with the little boats maintaining a noisy and colorful commentary on the incidents of the races. Another native sport is the «Canary wrestling», which was inherited from the old inhabitants of the islands. This type of wrestling is more than just a test of physical strength, but rather also a noble and virile display of ability and reflexes, which also includes moments of beauty provided by the gymnasts. In addition, on the level of spectacle sports, we must mention the greyhound races, the cock fights and the games of Basque jai alai; and in the area of active but restful sports, there are the many installations for bowling and mini-golf, among others.

A cockfight.

A moment in the original Canary wrestling.

THE NORTH: UNDER THE SIGN OF THE BANANA

By applying, to a certain extent, the hyperbole, we can say that the landscape of the North of Gran Canaria, and especially of its coastal area, is an invented landscape, created by man. Or, at least intensely remodeled by man. Of course, the climate has always collaborated favorably; but it is also true that man has had to deal with difficulty and danger with regard to two cardinal element: water and the land. In order to obtain water, it was necessary to make hundreds of holes in the ground of the island, forming a labyrinth of mines and galleries so that this precious liquid could be obtained more easily. With reference to the land, man was forced to curtail and care for it greedily, moving it, as if it were a rare mineral, from one place to another, sometimes over great distances. But the result —splendid and instructive— is easily seen, from one end to the other of this northern county. And especially on the wide coastal strip we find the vegetational symphony of green bounty-strong, vast, dominating; the brilliant emerald color of the banana trees. This part of Gran Canaria is one of the portions of our Planet dedicated to supplying the tables of European homes with this tasty fruit.

The banana is from Malasia, and it already existed in the Canary Islands in the XV century, principally as a decorative plaut for patios and gardens. About that time, it was taken to America and acclimatized on the island of Santo Domingo, extending to Cuba and finally to the continent.

However, the variety cultivated at present in the Archipelago is from Asia, and it seems to have been introduced in the Canary Islands by a French expedition that stayed here in 1855, on their return from Conchinchina. This variety is the only one generally grown at present, because of its quality, resistance and production.

The most important banana growing area on Gran Canaria is that of Arucas, the capital town of the area located in the center of a very fertile valley. This city is principally characterized because of its neatness and the beauty of its gardens which include the outstanding Municipal Park, a true showcase of exotic flowers and plants. Its parish church, although built in the last century, is in the pure Gothic style and this is not surprising (except for the chronological question) as it is located in this setting where the Tropics are hinted at with such strong characteristics. Next to the city we can see the volcanic cone known as the Mountain of Arucas, on the top of which there is a very modern and elegant tourist parador. From the terraces of this parador we can contemplate a series of wonderful panoramas, including a view of the Puerto de la Luz and the mountains of La Isleta. There is a highway that leaves Arucas in the direction of Teror, the village which owes its fame to the fact that it contains the sanctuary where the Virgin, Patron Saint of the Diocese, Nuestra Señora del Pino (Our Lady of the Pine), is worshipped.

Collecting bananas, one of Gran Canaria's principal riches. ▶

THE NORTH (II)

The highway of the North, logically starting from the capital, branches off in Arucas. One of the branches goes to Moya, and the other continues on hugging the coast of the Island, towards Agaete and San Nicolás. Along the first route, we will at once come upon the village of Moya, famous for the softness of its atmosphere and for having been the birth-place of the poet Tomás Morales. A little before reaching this point, we can turn off toward Firgas, using the highway that starts in the area around the vineyards of Buen Lugar. In Firgas, in addition to admiring the in-teresting spots that surround the town, we can visit the spring with its famous drinking water, known by the same name.

From Moya, if we take the Guía road, we can go to Fontanales, a beautiful place full of trees and fountains. Returning to the main highway, we head for Los Tilos which is a lovely reminder of the great forests that long ago covered this county, and which some old literary text called «La Selva de Doramas» or «The Forest of Doramas», rather hyperbolically.

After passing Palmitar, Brezal and Santa Cristina, we come across the district of San Juan, in the limits of Guía de Gran Canaria, and at once, the road we are following joins the general North highway which we left outside Arucas, and now, along this route again, jumping, in our imagination, one step back, we continue our excursion along the coastal strip. We will first come to Cruz de Pineda and Bañaderos, then San Andrés and the Pagador. Here we just about begin the climb up the Cuesta de Silva, a hill that takes the highway up to the top over high escarpments. Nearby, we find the Cenobio de Valeron, formed by a group of caves lodged beneath the formidable eaves of lava. According to some people the natives used these natural cells for the «harimaguadas» or «guanche» girls who were temporarily isolated from the others to be conveniently fattened up, on a special diet, on the eve of their wedding. Others say that they were used simply as silos for storing grain and assuring the pre-servation of the crops. A third opinion is that they were used simultaneous-ly for both purposes. On the top of the nearby Mountain of El Gallego, there are the vestiges of a «Tagoror», a place used for gatherings by the native people.

As we pass through the places we have mentioned, the North highway offers us one of the most spectacular views available on Gran Canaria. This panorama takes in all the coast that runs, full of banana plantations, from San Felipe, a sector located there below at the very edge of the sea, to the beach of Las Canteras and La Isleta, which stand out in the back-ground against the deep blue of the horizon.

Partial view of Moya. ▶

◀ Arucas is the centre of the banana-growing zone.

THE NORTH (III)

We are nearing another of the banana emporiums: the towns of Guía de Gran Canaria and Gáldar, who, in the shade of the Pico de la Atalaya —«Midget Teide»—, look at each other from their respective locations, on each side of the expensive Vega Mayor, where every bit of land is covered with banana plantations. Before reaching Guía, we must stop, at two modest homes which are quite a distance apart and both of which are almost in ruins; one is in Las Tres Palmas, near to the Lairaga coast, and it is the birthplace of the sculptor José Luján Pérez, the creator of outstanding images that fill the old churches of the Archipelago. The other («Villa Melpomene») is in Llanos de Parra and it is famous because the French musician Camille Saint-Saens lived here at one time. We can take advantage of our trip through Guía in order to admire some of the best carvings of Luján Pérez venerated in the church in his home town, and also to taste the famous «queso de flor».

The city of Gáldar is of special historical and archeological interest as it was an important native settlement it was so important that the great chief (the Guanarteme) settled his court here. Within the city limits there are numerous material vestiges of the «guanche» culture, including the so called «Cueva Pintada» a cave in which we find the remains of varied geometric paintings done in white, black, grey and predominantly reddish brown. In the City Hall of this town there is a small exhibition of objects of great anthropological value, and in the patio of the same building, there is a one hundred year old «drago». We must also point out the Parish Church and the Playa Mayor as worthy of interest.

After Gáldar, passing San Isidro and the Llanos de Sardina del Norte, near the beach of the same name, we come in sight of Agaete, with its great maritime heritage. All its maritime prestige has been provided by the Port of Las Nieves, now reduced to serving the colony of «bajura» fishermen that live here under the protection of the Virgin of the Snows («Las Nieves»), whose image, contained in a valuable Flemish tablet, is worshipped in a delightfully picturesque hermitage. The beach of Las Nieves, with its boulders, its thick greyish sand and the high, steep cliffs of basalt surrounding it, gives the inexperienced visitor and undefinable feeling, a mixture of wild charm and slight fear; this fear is perhaps caused by the imposing bulk of the mountains of Guayedra, Tirma and Faneque and the wall of Los Andenes which serve as a Wagnerian back drop. In this part of the island we must also visit the Valley of Agaete, a long, zig-zagging canyon with banana, coffee, papaya, avocado trees and corn, etc. Here there is a spring with waters rich in iron which are very important because of their digesting and healing powers. As a result of this, there is a spa here and in another building, a very large hotel.

Guanche caves gf the Cenobio de Valerón, on Silva Hill (Guidebook).

Plaza Mayor of Gáldar.

◀ Panoramic view of the beautiful Lairaga coast.

Partial view of Agaete.

General view of the Port of Las Nieves.

A view of the Port of Las Nieves.

ECONOMY

The fact that these are islands and that they are physically far away from the mainland, has always weighed on the economy determining its very evident nature as a «differential factor» within the framework of the Spanish collectivity. This explains why exterior commerce and the cultivation of special fruits for export have been for a long time now the fundamental keys to the economy of the Canary Islands. Today, two other elements have come to join these in the direction of the projection and the dependency of foreign countries: large scale fishing with its industrial by products and tourism.

With regard to the fact that it supplies foreign markets, the agriculture of the islands has, until recently, been based on the one crop system, and in this way, during the centuries, one single product from the land has fully occupied the islander's initiative and energies. For this reason, he has suffered from the problems inherent to this type of system, and the consequences of the successive collapse of shift planting. They were: sugar cane (XV-XVI centuries); wines (XVII-XVIII centuries); the «cochinilla» (XIX century) and finally in the XX century, the banana, until, especially after the 30's, the idea of banana-tomato somewhat softened the risks of the one crop system. Recently this plan for variation has been intensified with the production of cucumbers, egg, plants, flowers, peppers, etc.

International commerce is vital for the Canary Island, which is why so much energy is put into it not only to supply for local requirements and to export some of its natural products to other markets, but also, and to a great extent, to organize the great mercantile network of traffic due to its excellent geographical situation. This all fatally provokes a state of complete openness characterizing the economy of the Archipelago, of which a significant example is the fact that it is a Free Port, so advantageous for the islanders, who do not consider it a prerogative but rather the appropriate administration for an undeniable geo-economic reality.

The nearness of the islands to the Sahara shoals determined the very important development which has taken place in the activities related to the fishing sector. With regard to tourism we should say that this is not new to the islands, but it is now beginning, in a massive and even spectacular way to become part of the life of the Archipelago. It is unique, in relation to the rest of Spain, in that it receives the bulk of its visitors in the winter, because of its exceptional climate. Industry exists on a very modest level, with one or two relatively important products (preserves and fish by-products, nitrogeneous fertilizers, cement).

Agricultural tasks at Gáldar.

Preparing tomatoes for export.

Fruit and fish, together with tourism, are the basis of the islands'
economy.

THE SOUTH: THE LAND OF THE SUN

The South of Gran Canaria is a land of ambivalent, paradoxical scenery: severe and voluptuous at the same time. Its sensual quality is a gift of the light, the air, the sky... Its aesthetic condition, a result of its nude, burned orography. Here, joined in fascinating unity, on one hand: frantic light, warm air created by the constant breeze a round, high sky; and the sea «the great sea of frenzied rapture» as in the poem by Valery, a sea that rubs it slippery skin against the golden sands. On the other hand, the broken and, at times, convulsed geology, the omnipresence of the lava, on which the hands of man or the strong touch of erosion have left the balm of their prints... And in their respective seasons, alternating, the great victory, the absolute empire of only one of the two great elements of the synthesis: the sensual and the aesthetic. The first, at nigh noon; the latter, when the night announces its imminence.

But in one case as in the other, as at all times, these southern spots do not allow the traveller to be indifferent but they subdue or vex him depending on whether he is feeling tense or lax. «Tremendous skies», noted Carmen Laforet, the admirable novelist from the Canary Islands, when writing about the archipelago; «tremendous skies, crepuscular skies, the color of blood or of violets, envelop the afternoon. At noon the rocks tremble, evaporating into a golden mist. When night falls, the heat still remains in the quiet waters of the sea, which shines in the reflection of the heavy, large, low stars. The silhouettes of the teasels are strangely outlined in this clear sky and in the heat they look like green flames. There is no way to escape or to take the middle road. I know of those who hate this desolate landscape. I also know of those who, like myself, love it violently and without reservations».

It is natural that this scenery is not as pleasant for those who, by tradition or because of destiny, are involved in the basic trades of the area which are agriculture —tomatoes, cucumbers, potatoes, etc.— and fishing: these trades are continually being deserted by the younger generations who find a growing attraction for tourism and all connected activities. It is precisely the southern coast that represents the most spectacular development experienced in this industry on Gran Canaria. A complex network of installations and establishments of all kinds is slowly changing, with a variety of attractions, the place that, not long ago was a wild area, almost unapproachable for the traveller who landed on Gran Canaria, and even for its own inhabitants. One advantage of this sector is that all these projects are being carried out without harming the beauty and outstanding qualities of the area although an attempt is being made to harmonize refined comfort with a respect for the singularly attractive natural features.

Laboriously made water conduits are indispensable in the bare mountains of the south.

The Cortijo del Oasis, at Juan Grande.

THE SOUTH: WARM MIDWAY POINTS

Leaving Las Palmas, a visit to the lands of the South can be made in three directions. We can choose the beach route, following the highway from the Airport of Gando and its continuatión to Mogan, which is the general southern highway. Along this route, in addition to the beaches, we can see the extensive tomato flatlands of Carrizal, Sardina del Sur, Aldea Blanca and Juan Grande, and before, in Tufia, we find some remains of «guanche» constructions. On the level of Juan Grande, we can catch sight of the «Cortijo del Oasis», or ranch, one of the most delightful examples of the rural architecture of the Archipelago. Or we can follow the road which leads from Telde, to San Mateo de Tejeda, passing through Valse-

A characteristic landscape in the south («La Era del Cardón»).

quillo. And, fillally, we can head for the county of Los Tirajanas, in lands of the warm midway points of the «old island». Going in this direction, we first come upon Jinamar a small rural village rising amidst orchards planted in the «bad lands». At once, we come to Telde, the second largest town on the island after the capital, it is a very ancient hispanic settlement and in the distant past it played a very important part in the lives of the guanches. Here we can see the altarpiece in the Parish church of San Juan, which is a beautiful example of Flemish art, and the Christ of the High Altar in the same church, a very strange XVI century work, attributed to de Tabasco Indians (Mexico). There is also the neighborhood of San Francisco, with its old, charming appearance and heavy silence. On the road again, near El Goro, we pass the Mountain of the Four Passes, so named because of the number of approaches to the enclosure excavated there which was used as a «guanche» funeral ceremony ground. And we now come to Ingenio —a land of tomatoes and fine embroidery— with its solid, white church. Near Ingenio, we have opposite, the village of Agüimes, which in times past, was the domain of the Archbishops of the Islands. Continuing on our way, we comme upon Temisas, a very lovely small village, hidden among the nopal and olive trees, with houses miraculously untouched by cement. And after many turns and bends in the highway, we can suddenly see Tirajana. The county of Tirajana, or more correctly, Los Tirajanas, occupies the broken basm of a huge crater, located at the foot of the tall group of central peaks, and spreads out toward the coast, through a tormented geological panorama. Making fun of such scenography, the islander has known how to transform this vicious area of Gran Canaria into a flower garden: and in this way we find all over, in Santa Lucía and San Bartolomé de Tirajana, orchards of plums, apricots, cherries, and corn fields, etc. Santa Lucía de Tirajana surprises us unexpectedly with its small ethnological museum which was created as a result of the enthusiasm of don Vicente Sánchez Araña. A quick visit to the area of Fataga, delightfully intimate and quiet, will put the final touches to our excursion, and we now turn in search of the general southern highway which wil take us back to Las Palmas or to Maspalomas.

The enchanting district of San Francisco, in Telde.

Telde. Gothic-Flemish reredos in St. John's parish church. ▶

Guanche caves in the mountain of the Four Gates, at El Goro.

Santa Lucía de Tirajana. Entrance to «La Fortaleza» Ethnological Museum.

A beautiful landscape near Arinaga.

Scenery of the *medianías*, in the outskirts of Fataga.

THE SOUTH: THE BEACHES

With regard to tourist attractions, the South of Gran Canaria has come to mean the apotheosis of the beaches. From La Laja, in the area around Las Palmas, to Mogan, in the «old island» sector, the whole southern coast is a row of beaches. Small beaches or large ones; open or hidden ones; some strongly hinting at the fascination of the southern Pacific shores; all covered with inviting, fine, golden sand, such as, la Garita, Melenera, Ojo de Garza, Vista Alegre, Vargas, El Cardón, Tarajalillo, Morro Besudo, San Agustín, Bahía del Inglés, Maspalomas, Las Meloneras Arguineguín, Patalavaca, Puerto Rico, Tauro, Taurito, Mogán, Veneguera, etc. From among these, we must make special mention of those that form the complex of Maspalomas, which is 53 kilometers from Las Palmas and 28 from the Airport, covering a 17 kilometer area of beaches. They are called San Agustín, Playa del Inglés and Maspalomas itself, in addition to other smaller ones. San Agustín is quite small and is located in an area of perpetual calm. An intelligently constructed urbanization, on the basis of numerous gardens, scattered groups of bungalows, very modern hotels, pools and entertainment centers, all designed for the greatest comfort has converted this point into an important tourist attraction center on an international level. The Playa del Inglés is a vast strip of very fine, golden sand gently sloping down into an always blue and quiet sea. The Beach of the Faro, or called Maspalomas, is an extension of the Playa del Inglés and together they form the Parchel de las Nieves or the delta of the Barranco de Maspalomas. It consists of a flat extension of golden sands that rest on two adjacent and parallel levels: the beach itself, which is about six kilometers long, and the dunes, covering an area of approximately 250 hectareas and closely resembling the Sahara. This territory of dunes, with its curves that are sometimes visibly moving, with its tops and basins, is covered in sections with small thickets of tamarisk trees and xeric vegetation. Accentuating even more its resemblance to the Sahara (which however a soft trade wind hastens to cancel out), there is also a large and dense oasis formed by palm trees and marshes; and near the oasis, a small lagoon, where it is possible to fish and row about in small canoe-like boats. In some places along the edge of this pond, spread out attractively around the palm grove, we find the apartments and bungalows representing the first phase of an ambitious plan to urbanize this beach. It will also include sports fields, stadium, hypodrome, bull ring, etc. Almost all these buildings and areas will be situated at a convenient distance from the beach, not far from the hotel, together with the golf course and stables which are already in use. Both here as well as in San Agustín and Playa del Inglés, rainy or cloudy days are practically non-existent at any time of the year.

San Agustín beach.

San Agustín coast.

Inglés Beach. Hotel ensemble.

Inglés Beach.

The Oasis of Maspalomas is one of the most important tourist centres in the world.

Golf in the "Oasis Maspalomas".

CLIMATE, PLANTS AND WILDLIFE

The climate is the most important feature the Canary Archipelago
has to attract the imagination and will of so many people. A large amount
of travel literature or commentaries testifies this, ranging from Plutarch
to inexperienced newspapermen; this does not include the more formal
information given in scientific tests and official publications. The wonderful
Canary Islands are certainly not a mythical creation but rather a reality
which anyone can verify for themselves throughout the year. The oceanic
location of the Archipelago, its situation in the range of the trade winds,
the relief of the islands, and the so called «cold Canary current» (which
keeps the temperature on the surface of the water below what is normally
expected in this latitude), coincide and mix in the right proportions to
form the very singular climate of this part of the Earth. We can say —as
others have said over the centuries— that the Canary Islands enjoy a
never ending Spring.

Without a doubt, the most interesting aspect of the Islands' natural
landscape is the fauna which is so valuable and so varied that it has been
placed among the most outstanding in the area of phytogeography. Contributing factors include not only the long list of species which belong
to the Archipelago, but also the large portion of the world's plants which
have been acclimated here to form a truly complete garden. With reference
to native plants, the islands offer a special feature, consisting of a showcase
of species which are survivors of the European vegetation of the Third
and Fourth Periods, which died out of their original locations as a result
of the glaciers. They emmigrated to the islands in search of a more adequate
setting. Within the framework of original vegetation, we must mention,
for example: the «drago», a longeval tree with a disquieting appearance;
the Canary pine, very tall and hieratic; the island palm («phoenix canarien-
sis») which is characterized because of its straight trunk and the harmonious
radiation of its palm branches; the «cardon» or teasel which is a kind
of cactus whose thorny-edged stalks curve upward from the ground, forming
a shape somewhat similar to a gigantic candelabrum; the very beautiful
«taginaste», the «tabaibas», the «verodes», etc., etc.

On the other hand, if we exclude the varied and abundant marine
species, the chapter on animal life is of little interest. The most outstanding
in this area are two delightful songbirds: the «mountain canary» a distant
relative of the greatly sophisticated canaries which sing and are bred throughout the world; and the «capirote» a favorite with the native Canary
islanders; it is a small bird whose sweet, warm singing has for a long time
lent charm to many of the lonely places on the islands.

The vegetable world of the Canaries is of surprising richness and variety (Pines at Gáldar and palms at Santa Brigida).

Examples of the island flora: cactus and *tajisnaste*.

THE CENTER: WITH FOREST AND MOUNTAINS

The island of Gran Canaria, as seen from the coast in the direction of its geographical center which is at the same time its maximum height, is considered divided into there large areas, each with its own, individual personality: the coastal area (an altitude up to 300 meters), the midway area (from 300 to 950 meters) and the peak area (beginning at 950 meters).

The area we have included under the title of Center takes in practically all the middle zone in relation to the geologically named «new island». This area, to a certain extent cool and cloudy because of its exposure to the damp winds, was at one time completely covered by a forest and this is the reason for the patches of dark green in sections, not only in the valleys and ravines but also on the slopes and cliffs.

Leaving Las Palmas in one of the many confortable and economical means of transportation available, we can take a series of interesting trips which we shall outline here.

1) *LAS PALMAS-TEJEDA* — Via the Central highway, we very soon reach Tafira, Monte Coello and Monte Lentiscal, residential sectors located in the heart of the land nearest Las Palmas. Its landscape is a mixture of the strong urban features, the industrial crops of flowers, the palm trees and the private gardens. Its climate is without a doubt the most pleasant on the island, an indication of its superior position. Nearby we find the Valley of La Angostura, with the surging beauty of the vegetation and the crater and the peak of Bandama, with the bordering area full of vineyards which have been planted in the red and black volcanic sand covering the rolling, hilly ground. The crater or «boiler» of Bandama is an enormous bowl of reddish rock, with a radius of one kilometer and a depth of two hundred meters, at the bottom of which there are small plantations. Nearby, we have the Mountain of Los Lirios and the country house where don Benito Pérez Galdós spent part of his childhood, which still contains a number of personal reminders of the great novelist; and the Golf Club of Gran Canaria, which is a fine example with its excellent courses, located almost on the very edge of the «boiler», and the perfection and size of the installations.

In Tafira Baja we can visit the Jardín Canario a true, living botanical museum, dedicated to the preservation of the varied and interesting aboriginal plant life of this Area of the Atlantic.

If we keep on up the road we will come upon the towns of Santa Brígida and San Mateo, located in a bright area, rich in vegetation with lovely views of the mountains and the sea. Then we continue on towards Las Lagunetas, coming at once to the Cruz de Tejeda and the town of Tejeda at the vertex of the island, which we shall discuss in a later chapter.

The crater of Bandama. (Photograph by: C Enriquez de Salamanca).

THE CENTER: THE ROUTE OF THE ALMOND TREES

2) *LAS PALMAS-ARTENARA* —For this trip we must take the North highway to the crossroads of Tamaraceite where the road begins by taking us to Teror. We might say that in Teror the landscape of Gran Canaria has decidedly chosen the continental, European physiognomy, perhaps the Pyrenean, forgetting the Tropics. It is a land of corn fields and chestnut trees (the forest of Ossorio) of «ñameras» and poplar trees, and fruit or shade trees, of pools and light rain. These conditions also prevail in the next town of Valleseco which is permanently green and tender, in spite of its name («dry valley»). In Lanzarote, a section of Valleseco, which lies above the Balcón de Zamora, we begin to notice the strong mountain landscapes whilst the volcanic make-up once more dominates the island geology. From here, passing Cueva Corcho a place for sudden mists, we can easily reach Artenara and take in the unique spectacle of this town and the views from here. Almost every day you can see the very famous volcano, Teide, on the island of Tenerife.

3) *LAS PALMAS-TEJEDA, VIA VALSEQUILLO* —For this trip we must leave the city via the Southern highway, reaching the main plaza of the city of Telde; here we take the road leading directly to Valsequillo. This town is located in a large depression with the counterforts and imposing peaks of the central range nearby at the back of it. This range is situated between the northern and southern zones, halfway from the midway points and the coast. This is the reason for the unique quality of its landscape which combines rustic, almost wild features with chaste, fleetingly soft ones. The beauty of this landscape reaches its peak between the months of January and March when the thousands of almond trees in the Tenteniguada area and its surroundings burst forth in their vast and «silent cry of unanimous whiteness». From Tenteniguada, along a road which zigzags upward, we reach San Mateo, and from here to Tejeda, after having joined the route followed in itinerary one.

4) *THE ROUTE OF THE ALMOND TREES* —Valsequillo and Tenteniguada are not the only places where we can experience the always new and fascinating spectacle of the almond trees in flower, since the framework of the marvelous floral exhibition (which occurs here early, sometimes just a few days after the New Year) extends to almost all the vertex of the island and to the counterforts heading toward Valsequillo and San Mateo, on the one hand, and toward the gullies of Tejeda and the great valley of Tunte, on the other. Valsequillo, el Pedregal, Tenteniguada, San Mateo, Tejeda, Ayacate, San Bartolomé de Tirajana, the rocky places that serve as pedestals for the Nublo, Bentayga, Saucillo... present such a spell binding scene that even the least sensitive cannot fail to be bewitched.

◀ Partial view of the town of Santa Brigida.

Street with beautiful Canary balconies, and basilica of Teror.

Image of Our Lady of the Pine, Patron of the Island. ▶

A beautiful landscape: the patch of Tenteniguada.

Panoramic view from Artenara, in the central highlands of the Island.

THE VERTEX OF THE ISLAND

The shape of Gran Canaria, in relation to the two blue boundless spaces which are its setting (the first, an almost perfect cone rising rotundly up over an almost perfectly round base; the second two, the vast sea and the infinite sky), has proveked, in the fantasies of poets and non-poets, an enormous amount of imagery attempting to capture in metaphorical terms the surging form of the island and its oceanic spirit. Here are some of these lyrical definitions: «Balloon rocked by the winds», «Round cradle, rocked by the sea», «Pyramid of the ocean», «Inverted spinning top»... If we were to prefer the last of these images, we would have the point of the gigantic top, the island, formed by the spire of the Roque Nublo, that solitary and outlined peak of basalt that turns, not on the ground but 'in the sky, on the impulses of the double and simultaneous planetary revolutions.

We are at the vertex of Gran Canaria, at the point which is both the geographical center and the highest peak (1,950 meters). Here Nature carries to an extreme all the imposing features successfully tried out on other parts of the island. This is the dominion of the feverish stone, the setting for plutonic rage held for ever in a sequence of dramatic, twisted magnificence. Deep gullies, a jungle of gorges, precipices, jagged escarpments, plunging pinnacles, who vainly resist the biting teeth of erosion. «It is a tremondous upheaval from the bowels of the earth» commented Miguel de Unamuno, once a passionate visitor to the island, «it all resembles a petrified tempest; a tempest of fire and of lava, rather than of water».

Here we have Cruz de Tejeda and the National Tourist Parador the town of Tejeda, set in a fold of the land, in the midst of almond trees and orchards; Los Llanòs de la Pez, with its mountain refuge; Los Pechos, where we can contemplate the view of the southern county of Los Tirajanas. If we take the highway from Tunte through Ayacata, running quite close to the Pinar de Pajanales we can begin the descent in this direction. Here, in Tejeda there are the other rocks which together with the Nublo, keep the mountain watch: Bentayga, el Fraile, etc. Moving in a northeasterly direction, we soon reach Artenara, after circling round the crater of Los Pinos de Gáldar. Artenara is a little town hanging over the precipices of the Barranco de Tejeda. As a matter of preference or tradition rather than necessity, the majority of the town's population live in rooms excavated in the volcanic tuff. But these are not crude living quarters, but rather comfortable homes whose walls and ceilings, plain and whitewashed, look like normal houses on the inside. Also, in an underground room we find the vault and the altar of the Virgin of the town; the Virgin of the Little Cave, «La Virgen de la Cuevita». From Artenara, there are only eleven kilometers to the Pinar de Tamadaba, the vast remains of the dense forest which once, long ago, covered the island.

View of the National Tourist Parador at the Cruz de Tejeda, with the Cloudy Rock.

Entrance to the Parador at the Cruz de Tejeda.

Tejeda, with the Bentayga Rock. ▶

The centre of the Island has been described as a «petrified storm».

Chapel of the Virgin of the Little Cave,
at Artenara.

The Cloudy Rock and the Bentayga
Rock, with the Teide in the background.

THE «OLD ISLAND»

We have already insinuated that from the point of view of the genesis of the ground, Gran Canaria is considered to be divided into two great halves: the «new island», which was formed more recently (and is the larger part of the material already described), and the «old island» or portion of the Southwest, so called because it is geologically older. In this latter area the volcanic activity stopped before the other, and since then the change in its appearance has been almost exclusively due to the work of the erosive action of waters; the Canary islander, just the opposite from what has happened on the «new island», has hardly been able to attempt to domesticate these rough and surly natural features. This part of Gran Canaria is a craggy landscape, cut by deep ravines and pronounced elevations which, in some cases suddenly fall down into the ocean, forming sometimes unapproachable escarpments. It is also a land of extensive pine woods covering the peaks and the gullies of the island roof (Tamadaba, Iguana, Ojeda, Pajonales) and whose ever-green patches constrast sharply with the varied, flaming volcanic coloring of the ground. To a certain extent, the vision of these burned and wasted lands has been captured in «los poemas áridos» (The arid poems) of the famous lyric poet from Gran Canaria Alonso Quesada:

> *Fields, unplowed, eternal solitude*
> *—deep meditation on everything—.*
> *The sun beating down on the rocky cliffs*
> *and the sea... as if inviting the impossible!*

Leaving Agaete and after contemplating the large collection of impressive landscapes to be seen from the highway, especially after Guayedra and particularly from the Anden Verde, we come upon San Nicolás de Tolentino, a singularly hard working town which has come to be, like Mogan, a pioneer in the task of the positive taming of this part of Gran Canaria. Following the route around the island, we find, after short detours, the sectors of Tazarte, Tazartico and Veneguera, ideal for fishing, and then the Mogan area, a place whose name brings to mind thick tropical juices, like the pulp of many of its fruit, representing the most beautiful victory of the determination of the islanders, always at war with Nature who is constantly testing their capacity for self-denial and inventiveness. Next we have Arguineguín, a town of fishermen which has already been constructively incorporated (beach of Patalavaca) into one of the best tourist complexes on Gran Canaria. And from here we finally take up the South highway which, following an itinerary opposite to the one we have just noted, leads us from Las Palmas to Maspalomas.

◀ The murmuring Pine Forest of Tamadaba.

Beach of San Nicolás de Tolentino, in the west of the Island.

The valley of San Nicolás, in the *Isla Vieja*.

Tourist development at Puerto Rico.

Port of Mogán, in the south-west of the Island.

LANZAROTE, THE ISLAND OF VOLCANOES

The island of Lanzarote has one of the most unusual landscapes on the Earth and is without a doubt the most interesting of all the Canary Archipelago. Its outstanding unique quality is the result, to a great extent, of the intensive volcanic eruptions which have occurred here over the years, most recently in the XVIII and XIX centuries. During these latter periods, the ground was devastated by the prolonged and violent activity of its many volcanoes, which remodelled the inside and outside of the island, making it resemble a faithful copy of the lunar physiognomy as imagined by man. Rows of craters (there are more than one hundred) fields of thick volcanic ash, torents of multicolored lava, twisted and tortured rocks, desolate ravines... And the flying sands which cross the island, from shore to shore, descend on its «jables» like a warm, golden rain which is not exactly lethal. And the buzzing tactile wind. And together with these elements which are so capable of arranging a Dantesque scene, there are those which contribute to the other, more pleasant, kinder side of Lanzarote. The sky is a delirious blue, the beaches are covered with unusual black, red, grey, golden, white, sands... and the intimate coves, the elegant swaying of the palms, and man. These men have been able to obtain green patches and profits from the volcano and have known how to soften the austere features of the calcinated parts with the simple, serious grace of their rural architecture. The man who plow the lava dust with yokes of dromedaries and have found out how to capture the night breeze to make the seeds germinate buried in the furrows of sand.

Lanzarote is the eastern-most island of the Archipelago. It is 68 miles from the Spanish Sahara and 115 from Las Palmas de Gran Canaria. A trip from this city takes about fifty minutes by plane and about six hours by boat, via a normal interisland service. It has a surface of 795 km² and quite a varied coast line with alternating rocky areas and cosy beaches. It is generally low although it has several mountainous counties but the peaks arenot very high; its highest point (the Peñas de Chache, in the Famara-Guatifay range, in the North of the island) does not reach 675 meters. Its population is 40,000 and its inhabitants are primarily concerned with agriculture (vegetables, grain, onions, grapes, some tobacco), fishing and its related industries, as well as those activities related to tourism, which is beginning to take on considerable importance here now.

The capital of the island —Arrecife— is a clean and pleasant city, with the gentility of a small maritime town, and is full of a desire to progress as can be seen from an economic as well as from a cultural aspect. Here we find comportable lodgings and abundant vestiges of its not very ancient history.

Modern tourist facilities at Patalavaca beach.

131

Partial view of the port of Arrecife de Lanzarote.

View of the capital of Lanzarote.

The castle of San Gabriel, in Arrecife de Lanzarote.

Camels and dromedaries are indispensable animals for works in the fields of ▶ Lanzarote.

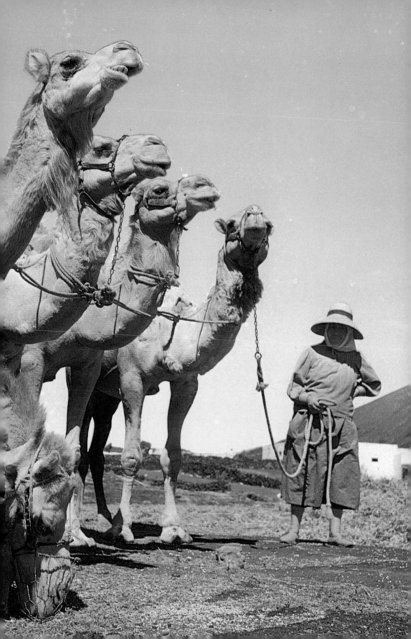

Harvesting onions, at Yaiza.

Monument to Fertility, by César Manrique, at Mozaga.

The windmill at Guatiza.

LANZAROTE (II)

THE NORTH ROUTE —Leaving Arrecife, with the towns of Ta-chiche and Nazaret behind us we come to Teguise, the old capital of the island. It is a priestly, aristocratic village where time seems to have stopped still. Its quiet atmosphere, the numerous churches and convents, the sight of the castle of Guanapay, the very names of some of its silent streets (i.e. the «Callejón de la Sangre»), all contribute to evoking the memory of old villages of Castile or some town of viceroyal America. Then we come upon Teseguite, with its wind mills, and Guatiza and Mala, near the Northeastern coast, where we find the bay of Arrieta and the beach of La Garita; then, heading inland toward the opposite shore, we suddenly catch sight of Haria and its valley full of palm trees. Then, Maguez and Ye, in the area which offers us two of the most interesting natural marvels of Lanzarote; the «jameos» and the Cave of los Verdes. The «jameos» are found in the county of Malpais de la Corona («malpais»: the badlands, area of modern lava) and are more or less deep ground cave-ins. The best known is the Jameo del Agua, with its subterranean lagoon inhabited by an unusual species of albino crab. The Cave of los Verdes is a wide volcanic tube, several kilometers long with a series of galleries and passages which have not as yet been completely explored. During the times when the island was the object of relatively frequent attacks by the Berbery pirates, the population sought refuge in this cavern. At present, lights have been installed highlighting the various colors of the rocks on the walls and ceilings. Finally, we must visit the Riscos de Famara and from its Vista del Río observation point, we can contemplate the rocks and tiny islands which complete the Archipelago, and among these we find La Graciosa, which we can reach by boat in a short time from the little port of Orzola.

THE SOUTH ROUTE —There is an amazing number of beaches on Lanzarote, especially along the southern coast of the island. Here are some of their names, from an unending list, beginning at the area around Arrecife: beach of Reducto, beaches of Guacimeta Playa Blanca (10 kilometers from the capital; information necessary to distinguish if from another place of the same name), Matagorda,. Los Pocillos, El Golfo, Las Mujeres, Las Coloradas, del Papagayo and Playa Blanca. Especially outstanding are the beaches Golfo and the second Playa Blanca. The first is located in a very beautiful volcanic landscape, occupying part of the crater which has been half devoured by the sea. The chromatic contrast of the ground and the water (blues and greens with a rich range of shades and hues) gives this sunny spot special charm. The Playa Blanca (in front of the little island of Lobos and the island of Fuerteventura) is the largest beach on Lanzarote and is outstanding because of its white sands and calm waters.

The Royal Town of Teguise, former capital of the Island, has important ▶ monuments.

Guanapay Castle, near Teguise.

The «African» valley of Haria.

Landscape in the valley of Haria.

The *Jameos* of the Water.

The volcanic beach of El Golfo.

The important salt-pans of the Janubio. ▶

Tourist development at Playa Blanca.

Partial view of Uga.

LANZAROTE (III)

THE CENTRAL ROUTE —Here Lanzarote offers the traveller the most unbelievable landscapes. On this part of the island, we can clearly see the struggle between man and Nature, shaken in the past by the Plutonic fury which can still be seen in the scars of the cataclysm. This battle was sometimes (miraculously?) won by man and at times he was reduced to complete uselessness, although almost without endangering his dynamic tenacity. And in this way, it is possible for us to contemplate places of complete desolation on which the claws of an apocalyptical beast still seem to be pushing and others where the volcanic domain is suddenly softened by the heroic green and the intense white of the rural constructions.

This route will take us, on the one hand, to San Bartolomé, Mozaga, Tao, Tiagua, Tinajo, Tajaste, Tinguatón, etc., and on the other, to Tías, Tegoyo, Uga, Yaiza and several others whose strange sounding names seem to underline the irreality of the landscape. And, above all, our eyes and the most hidden corners of our soul will be filled with the sights of La Geria de los Vinos and the hell of Timanfaya, places which it will be difficult to erase from the memories of all who set eyes on them.

La Geria is a large valley surrounded by volcanoes and covered with lava and black sand where the Lanzarote farmer has forced, one by one, fig trees and grape vines to grow, often in individual holes surrounded by stone walls to protect the plants (almost invisible) from the wind that whips this area.

The county of Timanfaya was the scene of the great eruptions on Lanzarote, between 1730 and 1736 and in 1824, completely levelling this part of the island, which was precisely the most fertile and tilled section. Towns, villages, farms, orchards, houses were materially erased from the face of the earth by the rage of the thirty volcanoes which all at once opened up their destructive mouths. At present, we donot have too have much of an imagination to vividly recall the terrible cosmic drama which took place here where the dominant feature continues to be the sight of the craters and the seas of twisted, multicolored lava. Absolute, terrifying silence hovers over this area which is bright and at the same time gloomy, where not even the least expression of animal or plant life is possible.

In Timanfaya we find the very famous Mountains of Fire, so called because they have a temperature inside of up to 400° and this heat can be felt even on ground level by digging a little in the earth. Especially on the little island of Hilario or the mound of Tenecheyde we can have a very unusual experience, further enriched by a pintoresque application: the cooking of food in the natural oven, the mountain. Our visit to Timanfaya has another attraction: the trip through its impressive lonely places on the back of slow, swaying dromedaries which, as we already know, are the most characteristic animals of Lanzarote.

The miraculous cultivation of vines at La Geria. ▶

Aspects of the Fire Mountains, at Timanfaya; Islote de Hilario; caravan of tourists riding slow dromedaries, and chapel of the Virgin of the Volcanoe.

FUERTEVENTURA: A SANATORIUM FOR THE SPIRIT

Anyone who comes up against a frivolous description of Fuerteventura might possibly decide to eliminate this island from his list of places to see during his visit to the Canary Islands. This would be a shame, especially if the prospective visitor has a refined spirit, capable of capturing the aesthetic beauty of the waste, barren areas. In Fuerteventura we will also feel the emotion of quiet times, of hours anchored in the backwaters of remote times which still seem to center on the life of some of these towns which are the color of the ground and which spring up from time to time in the valleys and on the plains with their frightening muteness. Lonely palm trees, wind mills, the flights of sparrow-hawks, the dromedary yoked to the incessant draw-well, the tall woman dressed in a long, loose black gown, walking slowly beside the small donkey; the biblical oven, the herds of goats, a well, the half destroyed tower... These are some of the images which are engraved on the minds and the sensitivity of the traveller who ventures into what Unamuno —with his maximum poetic definitions— called the «skeleton of the island». This island, in addition to the lyrical meditations of the great Basque, has inspired moving verses from some Canary island poets. But the time seems to have come to begin to rectify this image as over the last few years the first energetic steps have been taken to incorporate it into the arrangement of progressive collectivies. In this sense its most immediate goals are centered around certain specialized crops (tomatoes and sisal) and tourism. Its splendid beaches —the best on the Archipelago— provide it with excellent possibilities in this second activity.

Fuerteventura is divided into two sectors: the largest and inhabited one was historically called Mazorata and the second is the small peninsula of Jandía —facing Gran Canaria— where we find the highest peak on the island, the Pico de las Orejas (844 meters). Its territory, with very few hills, covers an area of 1,731 km², and is thus the second largest of the islands of the Archipelago. Its most interesting towns and places, southward, beginning at Puerto del Rosario, the capital of the island, are: Casillas del Angel. La Ampuyenta. La Antigua. Betancuria. Valle de Río Palma. Santa Inés.Tiscamanita, Agua de Bueyes, Tuineje. Pájara. Toto and Gran Tarajal. Northward, we find: which regard to beaches, near Puerto del Rosario, we find Playa Blanca and Puerto Lajas, later travelling from the south, along the Northeastern coast, the Matorral, Caleta de Fuste, Pozo Negro, Gran Tarajal, Tarajalejo, La Lajita and Matas Blancas. Then, on the peninsular sector; the large, superb solitary beaches of Sotavento de Jandía and Morro Jable. To the North, in front of the little island of Lobos. Corralejos is already a promising reality as far as the future of tourism on Fuerteventura is concerned.

Partial view of Puerto del Rosario, capital of Fuerteventura.

Corralejo, in the north of Fuerteventura.

Scenery of Vega de Río de Palma.

The lordly town of Betancuria, former capital of Fuerteventura.

Detail of the baroque portal of the parish church of Pájara.

Girl of La Oliva, in front of the House of the Colonels.

THE LITTLE ISLANDS... AND AGAIN THE FABLE

And at last we come to La Graciosa, the smallest of the inhabited islands. The word «island» is really too broad for La Graciosa and it would be more appropriate to call its physical entity (25 km²) a large rock or a tiny island. It is formed by a small number of volcanoes, and the entire coast is bordered by white sandy beaches. The other little islands (which are all situated at the head of Lanzarote, except for Lobos) are: Alegranza, Montaña Clara, Roque del Infierno (or del Oeste), Roque del Este and Isla de Lobos. This last one is located between Fuerteventura and Lanzarote, in an area known as La Bocaina, and covers approximately 7 square kilometers. Montaña Clara (1 km²) is formed by one volcanic cone open on one of its sides. The Roques are merely fragments of volcanoes which have already been crushed by the Atlantic waves. Except for La Graciosa and the Isla de Lobos, and to a certain extent Alegranza, the approach to these small islands is not at all easy.

This information on the Canary Islands in which we have included with some detail the eastern group and in which we have only touched on the group composing the Santa Cruz de Tenerife province, must contain just one more part. Paradoxically, this is an island which *is* but which does not exit. Or more precisely: which exists only in the geography of the imagination even though its part in the history of the Archipelago has left behind it definite facts and traces. We are referring to the island of San Borondón. A chimerical, movable, evading island, which used to emerge suddenly out of the ocean, tempting the navigators with its unknown secret just to disappear as suddenly as it appeared. This fable which formed an intense, part the islander's life for a long time is nothing more than another version of the legend of San Brandano, the VI century Irish saint who took to the water, down the Atlantic, on the back of a gigantic whale, in search of nothing less than Earthly Paradise. The only difference is that in the Canary version the place of the cetacean is occupied by a real island, with mountains, canyons, fascinating forests and with another feature that the other also very real islands would like, even though on a smaller scale, for themselves: a pair of wide, deep rivers as can be seen on the map drawn in 1590 by Leonardo Torriani. It still happens today as the press will, every now and then, report the re-apparance of this famous and thousands of years old serpent of the sea, which the old texts also called «Lost» «Enchanted» or «Deceitful». Here, in the XX century, the Canary Islands continue to be a frontier land of the fable, a country bordering on myth: this area of marvels where the physical and metaphysical planning of the islands has been going on for years and years and years.

La Lajita beach.

La Graciosa, from the Vista del Río, in the north of Lanzarote.

EVEREST

CALLEJERO
DE
LAS PALMAS
DE GRAN CANARIA

Editorial Everest, S. A.

MADRID • LEON • BARCELONA • SEVILLA • GRANADA • VALENCIA
ZARAGOZA • BILBAO • LAS PALMAS DE GRAN CANARIA • LA CORUÑA
PALMA DE MALLORCA • ALICANTE — MEXICO • BUENOS AIRES

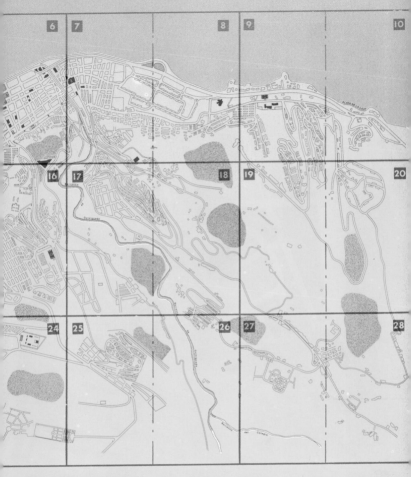

LAS PALMAS DE GRAN CANARIA
Escala 1 : 10.000

PLANO LLAVE
(dividido en 28 planos parciales)

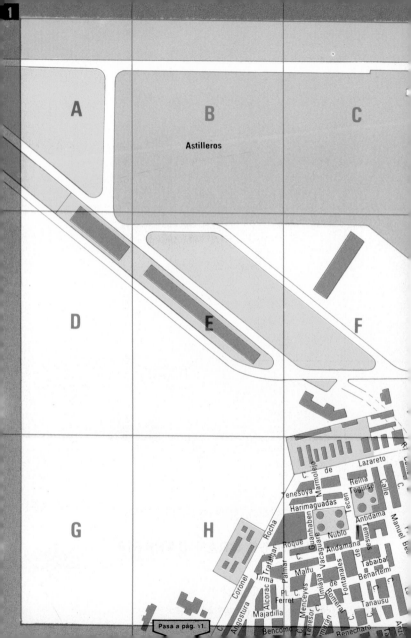

1

A

B

Astilleros

C

D

E

F

G

H

Pasa a pág. 11.

Lazareto

C. Reina Taguise Calle C.

Tenesoya

Marmolejo de

Harimaguadas

Antidama

Temisas

Manuel Be

Rocha

Roque

Guanhaben

Vacaguare

Nublo

Andamana

ap

Tabaibal

Benartemi

Coronel

Tirma

Palma

Malfu

Umiaga

Fontanales

Tanausu

Alcorac

Menceyes

de

Romeral

Angostura

Majadilla

Ferret

Tenesor

Umarán

Bencomo

Benecharo

Pl. C.

Trafalgar

Pl. C.

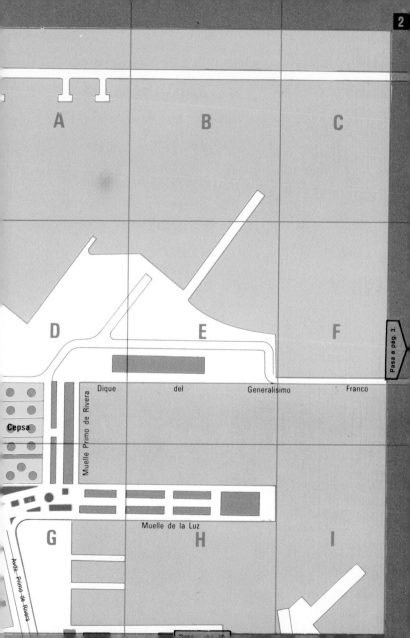

A

B

C

D

E

F

Pasa a pág. 3.

Dique   del   Generalísimo   Franco

Muelle Primo de Rivera

Cepsa

G

Muelle de la Luz

H

I

Avda. Primo de Rivera

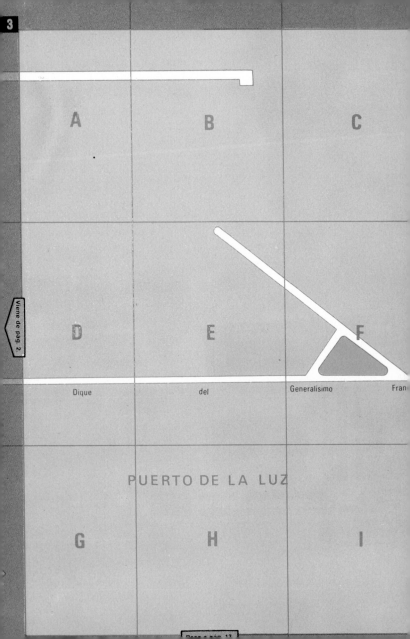

3

Viene de pag. 2

A

B

C

D

E

F

Dique   del   Generalisimo   Fran

PUERTO DE LA LUZ

G

H

I

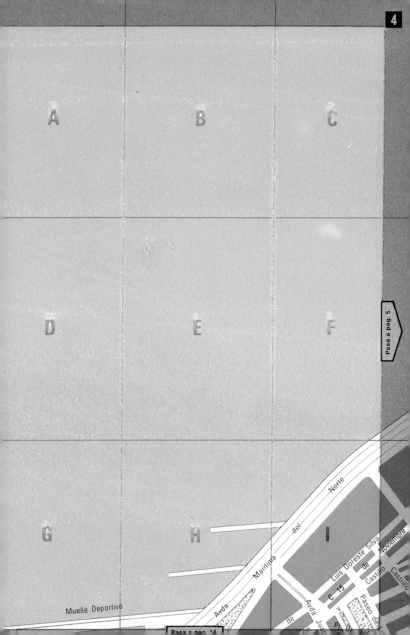

A

B

C

D

E

F

Pasa a pág. 5.

G

H

I

Norte.

Marítima

del

Avda.

Avda. Juar

de

C. 15

y

Luis Doreste Silva

de

Castillo

Paseo de

Pl. De

Castillo

Noviembre

Muelle Deportivo

Pasa a pág. 14

5

A

B

C

1.—Mercurio
2.—Madera
3.—Nieve
4.—Milagro
5.—Lago
6.—Limonero
7.—Dr. Manuel de La Nuez
8.—Moneda
9.—Malta

Viene de pág. 4.

D

E

Parque San Telmo

Avda.

Cal

Arrieta
de
Alonso

Venegas
Álvarado

Castillo
de Vera

Iberia

Colmenares
Bravo
Edua

Perojo

Plaza Pedro
P. Hilario C.

Canalejas

Navarro

Calle
y

Bosque
T.
Iriarte Peña

Comandancia Marina

Calle
Noviembre

León

Plaza de
La Feria

Calle
de
Jaime

Murga
Balmes

Celbrián

Ra

de
15

Gobierno Civil

Plaza
Héroes del Alcázar

Eusebio

Senador

Castillo Olivares

Morales

Angel Guerra

Luis
Doreste
Silva

C.
A
Bethencourt
de

Viento
Musset

Doctor Waksman

M.
C.
Anido

Rabadán
Tomás

Morales

Luis de la Cruz
Chil
Arac

Molinos

de
Padrón
Pamochamoso

Aguaduce
Naranjo

Galo Ponte
Pl.
Perón

Alfonso
XII

Plaza de
Tomás Morales

E

Universidad Internacional

León Rich
M.
V.
M.
DR.
C.

C.
C.
M.

Calle

de
Calle

G

C. de
Chapas

Matías
de

Suárez
Angel

Carvajal

Gumera

Obispo Encina

Jerónimo de Falcón

del
Toro

Paseo
del

Ladera de Cuyas
Subida a Schamann
Guerra

SAN A

Paseo de B

Pasa a pág. 15

A

B

C

Canarias

de

Saavedra

Alcalde Díaz

Doreste

Plaza
Santa Is

San
Agustín

Morera

Rutindana

Ceron

Quintero

A. Millares

Alcalde Fco. Hdez. Glez.

Pedro

de Sosa

Cabrera

Mataderó

Mies

Mendizábal

Oca Audiencia

Doctor

Espíritu

Dolores

Domingo

la

José

de

Rocha

Calle

Botas

Mercado

C.

Calvo Sotelo Balcones

León

Algaba

C. F. Massieu T.

C.

Reyes

Rosario

Galindo

Alonso

Católicos

Pl. F. Jareño

Stagno

Lentini

Herrería

Molino

Obispo

Reloj

Catedral

Dtor

Verneau

García Tello

A.

San

Marcos

Galván

Pérez

Montauder

de Viana

San Pedro

Mendoza

Pl. H

Codina

Plaza
Santa Ana

**Museo
Canario**

Luis

Millares

Toledo

Dtor Núez

Dtor.

San Francisco

Gourie

Triana

Peregrina

Pl.

Cairasco

Muro

Terrero

Fuente

San Diego de Alcalá

Dorama

Pl. Espir

Sto.

Domingo

Pl. Sto.

Correg.

Agu

Cano

A.

Colón

San Nicolás

Justo

Quesada

Sta Bárbara

Hernán

S. Calde

Lagunetas

Arena

Gral. Manninra

Dr. Deniz

Artiles

Mr.

Alcalde

Jordán

López Botas

Pedro Díaz

Sta Brígida

D. V. Ramírez

D. J. R.

Dide

Clavijo

Galdós

San Bernardo

Padilla

de

Mayo

Concha
Espina

Blisse

Verdi

Castillo

Paseo

Cal. S. Vicente

Aurora

San J

Doctor

1.º

Juan

Minerva

Guerra

Girasol

Río S. Nicolás

Gabarra

Globo

Galán

Ramón y

Real

B. Lis

Candil

Aires

Troya

Domingo

Rueda

Nogal

Rosal

Lima

del

Milagro

3 4 5 6

9 8 7

Cajal

Bretón

Pasa a pág. 7

Venus

Saturno

Sirena

1 2

SAN FRANCISCO

Pedro Quintana

Real

Álamo

Galera

Turia

Segura

Verona

Granata

Cecelia

Castillo

de

S. Roque

Carretera del

D

E

F

SAN BERNARDO

SAN NICOLAS

del

Barranco

Juan Jazmínero

SAN LAZARO

Antonio

Carretera

de

Camino

Real

del

Castillo

Callejón del Molino

de

Guiniguada

Carretera del

G

**Castillo de
S. Francisco**

H

Av. Palvorín

Mata

Urb.
S. Francisco

SAN ROQUE

Foro

Fama

Frayuca

Flecha

Fresa

Pasa a pág. 16.

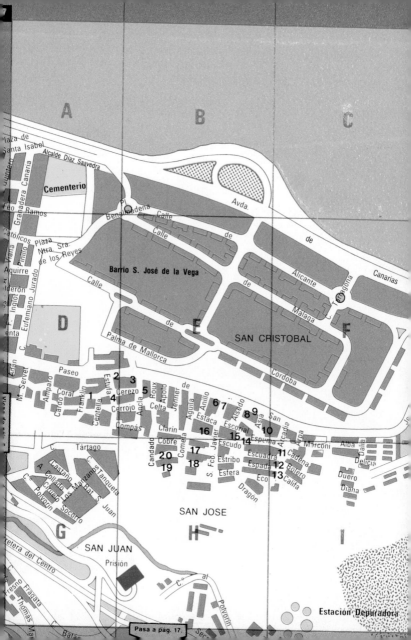

A B C

Plaza de
Santa Isabel
Alcalde Díaz Saavedra
Granadera Canaria
Cementerio
Fco. Ramos
Avda.
Pl.
Benalmádena
Calle
Católicos Plaza
Ntra. Sra. Calle de
Pinillo de los Reyes
Aguirre
Calle
Iderón
Calle de Alicante
Barrio S. José de la Vega
Eufemiano Jurado
Palma de Mallorca
de Málaga
Tarragona
Canarias

D E SAN CRISTOBAL F

Paseo
Córdoba
M. Servet
Amparo
Coral 2 3
Franklin Estrella Cerezo 5 Roux de
Cardón Centella 1 4 Ancla Celta Apolo Jenner Aguila Anillo 6 7
Cerrojo Clarín Estaca Arsedo 8 9
Compás 16 Escorial 15 14 Espuña 10
Candado Cobre Corneta 17 Escudo Alcadia 11 Cadena
Tártago 20 18 S. Fco. Javier Estribo Escuadra 12 Bolero
19 Espada 13 Califa
Tanqueta Esfera
Castaño Los Manzano Bat. S. Juan Eco
A Collado Los Dragón
Cueto Socorro
Polvorín

SAN JOSE

G H I

SAN JUAN
Prisión

Carretera del Centro

Estación Depuradora

Pasa a pág. 17.

Pasa a pág. 9.

Pasa a pág. 18.

9

A

B

C

Viene de pág. 8.

Avenida

D

E

F

de

Antigua

C. Pepe

Brahms

Miguel Gil

carretera

Cañarias

PLAYA DE LA LAJA

Sarg. Salom

Álamo

R. Urrutias

Timimi

del

Calle

Sur

C. Juan

Dvorac

de

Hoya

de

la

Plata

Sebastián

C.

Cantábrica

José

Quintana

Bach

C.

Presa

de

León

Amador

Suárez

De Bussy

Schubert

C. María

Obispo Albiturria

G

Subida a Pedro Hidalgo

Paralela a Pedro Hidalgo

H

I

Urbanización Hoya de la Plata

PEDRO HIDALGO

C.

Palencia

Pasa a pág. 19.

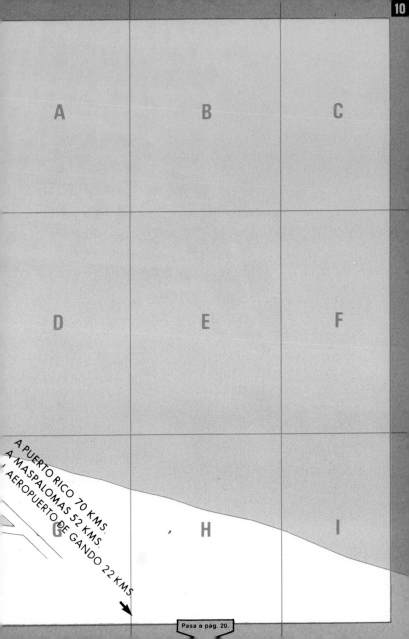

A

B

C

D

E

F

A PUERTO RICO 70 KMS.
A MASPALOMAS 52 KMS.
AEROPUERTO DE GANDO 22 KMS

G

H

I

Pasa a pág. 20.

Viene de pág. 1.

A

B

NUEVA ISLETA

Urbanización
Nueva Isleta

D

F

1.—Los Claveles
2.—J. Garay
3.—Rafael Bento Travieso

G

H

I

C. Rocha
C. Anglistura
Majadilla
Bencomo
Mencejas
Tenesor
Tamarán
Benchara
C. Guadarfía
Guayedra
de
C. Fontanales
C. de
C. de Sen
C. Bandama
Arauz
Osorio
Elcano
Artemi
C. Aremoga
Fataga
Tamadaba
Palmar
Los Fáicanes
Juncalillo
C. del
Tejeda
Tauro
Tecen
Pere
Silva
Calle
Pinzones
Faya
Coronel
Salvago
Almagro
Bentaguaire
Petojta
Guayre
Taliarte
Serdeto
Amaran
Acero
Tajaste
Adargoma
Guanchía
Benteuri
C. de
Princesa
Chyans
del Pardilla
Magallanes
Pl. del Pueblo
Ines
Avacata
Saucillo
Tenteniguada
Tostana
Timbaba
Bentayga
Luna
Lujan
Guayadeque
C. de
Torenburu
C. Ramos
Calle
Mayorazgo
Safaute
C. Hnos de
Blas
Gamonal
Valsendero
Jorge Marrero
de
Bentagache
Aguatona
Calle R. Manrique
C. A
Lezo
Timagan
Entrada Factoría

Viene de pág. 2.

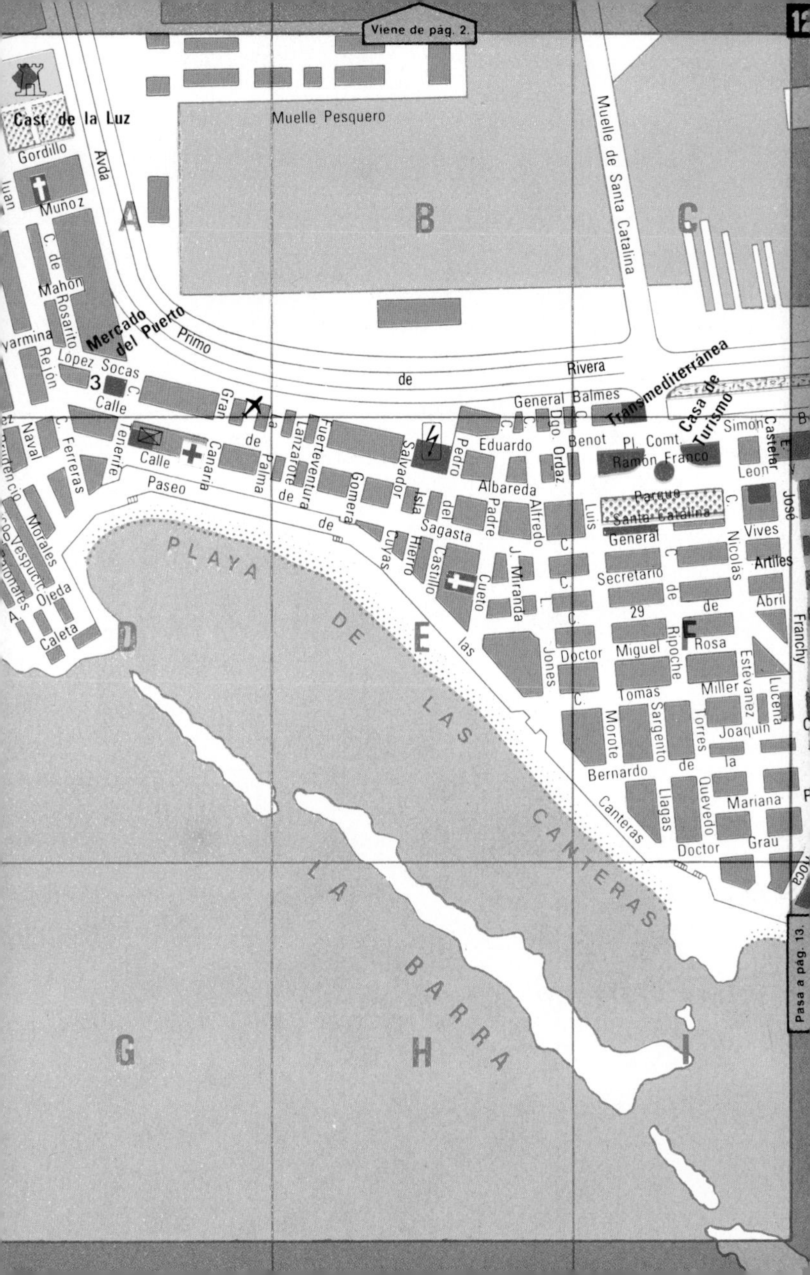

Cast. de la Luz

Gordillo

Juan

Muñoz

A

C. de

Mahón

Rosarito

yarmina

Retón

Lopez Socas

3

Calle

Tenerife

Ferreras

Calle

Morales

Ojeda

Caleta

D

Navas

mercio

Morales

Vespucio

ronautas

A.

Avda

Muelle Pesquero

B

Muelle de Santa Catalina

C

Mercado del Puerto

Primo

de

Rivera

General Balmes

Transmediterránea

Casa de

Turismo

Calle

Gran

Canaria

de

la

Palma

X

Gomera

Salvador

Lanzarote

de

Fuerteventura

Isla

Hierro

Pedro

Eduardo

Padre

Castillo

Cuyas

Sagasta

Albareda

Alfredo

J. Miranda

Cueto

Luis

Benot

Ordaz

Dao.

Pl. Comt.
Ramón Franco

Parque
Santa Catalina

General

Secretario

Simon

Castelar

Leon

Vives

Nicolás

de

29

de

Rosa

Doctor

Miguel

Ripoche

F

Estevanez

Jones

Tomas

Miller

Morote

Sargento

Torres

Joaquin

Bernardo

de

Quevedo

la

Llagas

Mariana

Doctor

Grau

PLAYA

DE

LAS

CANTERAS

Paseo

Canteras

E

G

LA

BARRA

H

I

Simon

José

Artiles

Franchy

Abril

Lucena

C

P

Pasa a pág. 13.

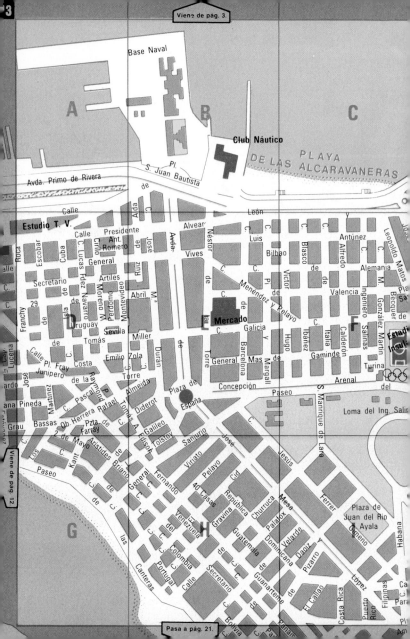

3

A

Base Naval

B

Club Náutico

C

PLAYA DE LAS ALCARAVANERAS

Pl. S. Juan Bautista

Avda. Primo de Rivera

Calle

León

y

Estudio T. V.

Calle

Presidente
Ant. Romero

Alvear

Néstor

Luis

Antúnez

Leopoldo Matos

Roca

Escobar

Cuba

C. Lucas Fdez Navarro

Cirilo

de

José

Avda.

Vives

de

C.

Bilbao

Blasco

de

Víctor

Alfredo

de

Alemania

M.

Becquer

Secretario

General

Artiles

Ruiz

Mª

Menéndez y Pelayo

Pl. de

Valencia

Ingeniero

González Martín

Salinas

Plaza

Franchy

29

de

de

Moreno

Montevideo

Abril

de

C.

C.

Galicia

Hugo

Ibáñez

Italia

Calderón

Martín

E **Mercado**

D

Uruguay

W

Sevilla

Miller

Torre

Mas

de

Gaminde

F

Estadi Insul

de

Tomás

Duran

Barcelona

Margall

Costa

Emilio Zola

de

General

Arenal

Turina

Calle Pl. Fray

Raymund

Concepción

Paseo

del

José

Junípero

de la

Torre

Almeida

Plaza de

S. Manrique de Lara

Ana

Pineda

P.

Diderot

España

Loma del Ing. Salir

Grau

Bassas

Ob. Herrera

Rafael

Tomás A. Edison

Galileo

Tolstoy

Sanurio

José

Jesús

los

de Mayo

C.

Arístides de Briano

Venezuela

Viriato

Pelayo

Cid

Ferrer

ardo

Kant

General Fernando

40 Casas

República

Churruca

Mesa

Plaza de
Juan del Río
y Ayala

Cigüeño

Paseo

de

las

Colombia

Gravina

Guatemala

Palafox

Velarde

Dominicana

Daoiz

Pizarro

Habana

G

Canteras

Portugal

Calle

Secretario

Guanarteme

El Callao

Costa Rica

Puerto Rico

Filipinas

H

Bolivia

Viene de pág. 12

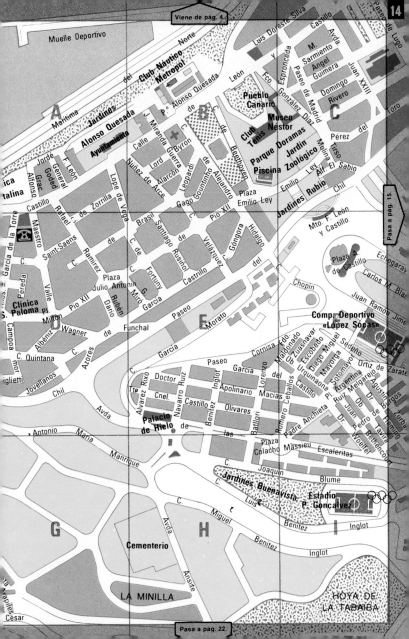

Viene de pág. 4.

Pasa a pág. 15.

Muelle Deportivo

Club Náutico Metropol

Jardines Alonso Quesada
Ayuntamiento

A

Pueblo Canario
Museo Néstor
Club Tenis
Parque Doramas
Jardín
Piscina Zoológico

Jardines Rubió

C

Paseo de Lugo

Castillo
Luis Doreste Silva
M. Sarmiento
Angel Guimerá
Juan XXIII
Domingo Rivero
Fco. Esproncedo
Paseo de Madrid
León
González Díaz
Toro
del
Pérez
Tirso
Molina
Alf. El Sabio
Emilio Ley
Chil
Mto. F. León y Castillo

P. Alonso Quesada
de
Calle
J. Miranda Guerra
Byron
Lord
de Beethoven
C.
Núñez de Arce
Leopardi
de Alejandro
Gago Goutinho
Velázquez
Pío XII
Brasil
Hidalgo
del
Góngora
Castrillo
Plaza Emilio Ley

Jordé
F. León
Gral. Godet
General Alfonso
Castillo
Maestro
García de la Torre
Saint-Saens
C. de Zorrilla
Ramírez
Lope de Vega
Rafael
C. de
Santiago Rusiñol
C. de
Fortún
G. García
Plaza Julio Antonin
Pío XII
Rubén Darío
Miró
C.
Paseo
Morato

Chopin

Plaza A. de Castillo
Echegaray
Carlos M. Blat
Juan Ramón Jimé

Clínica Paloma
Pereda
Valle
Milton
Albéniz
Wagner
Azores
de
Funchal
Jovellanos
Chil
Quintana
Campoa
mor
iglietti

D

C. García

E

Comp. Deportivo «López Socas»

Ob. Zuasnavar
Escobedo
Diego Miguel Sedeño
Mayorga
Ortiz de Zárate
Agustín
Burgos
Zurba
Maldonado
Urquinaona
Castillo
del
Pl. Argentina
Sotomayor
Ob. de Fleming
Bethencourt
Avenida
Dr. Woelfel
Juan Pedro
Cornisa
Paseo García
Lorenzo
del
Ceballos
Romero
Padre Anchieta
Plaza Colacho
Massieu
Escaleritas

Doctor
Apolinario
Macías
Olivares
Inglot
Battllori
Mejarejo
Ruiz
Tte. Álvarez Rixo
Cnel. Navarro Ruiz
Castillo Benítez
Palacio de Hielo
de
las

Avda.
Antonio
María
Manrique

Joaquín
Blume
Jardines Buenavista
Estadio P. Goncálvez
C. Luis
Benítez
Inglot

G

H

Cementerio
Avda.
Miguel
Benítez
Ansite

I

L

LA MINILLA

HOYA DE LA TABAIBA

Pasa a pág. 22.

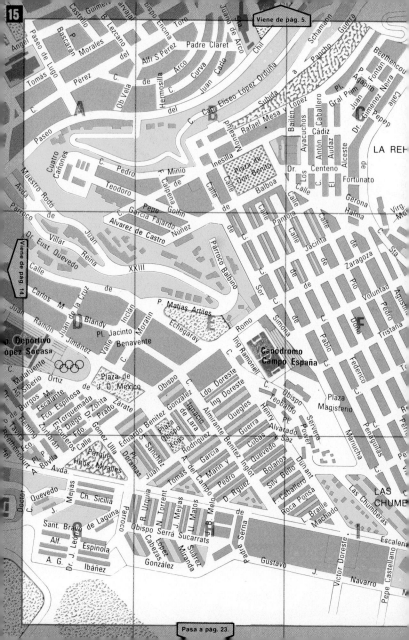

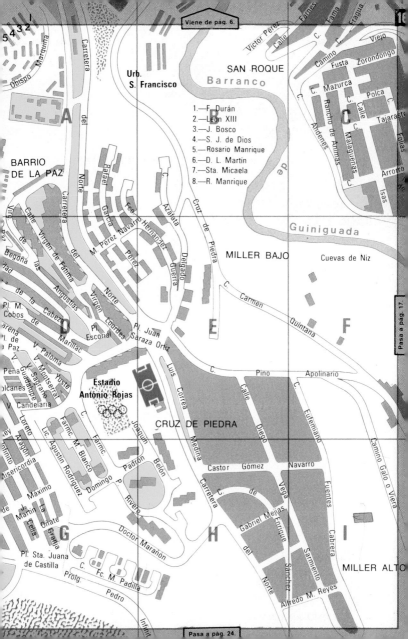

Viene de pág. 6.

1

5 4 3 2 1

Obispo

BARRIO
DE LA PAZ

Carretera

del

Norte

Virgen de las

Begoña

Calle Virgen de Fátima

de la Cabeza

Pl. M.
Cobos

Marillac

arena
l. de
a Paz

V. Paloma

Peña

V. Segrada

Guadalupa

Montserrat

Yuste

olcanes

V. Candelaria

ley

Loreto

Aragón

Misericordia

Maximo

J.
Martin

Celia

Oñate

Granja

Pl. Sta. Juana
de Castilla

Prolg.

Pedro

Infinit

Urb.
S. Francisco

A

Rafael García

M. Pérez Navarro Hernández

Norte

Peñer

Angustias

V.

D

Pl.
Escorial

Pl. Lourdes

Pl. Juan
Saraza Ortiz

Estadio
Antonio Rojas

⊙⊙⊙⊙⊙

C.

Farmc.
Mª Blanco

Lic. Agustín Rodríguez

Domingo

Padrón

P.
Rivera

Joaquín Belón

Doctor Marañón

C. Fc. M. Padilla

G

B

1.—F Durán
2.—León XIII
3.—J. Bosco
4.—S. J. de Dios
5.—Rosario Manrique
6.—D. L. Martin
7.—Sta. Micaela
8.—R. Manrique

C.

Azfata

Delgado

Cruz de Piedra

Guerra

E

Cruz de Piedra

C.

Luis Correa

Medina

Carretera

Castor Gómez

C. de

Gabriel Mejías

del

Enrique

Norte

SAN ROQUE

Barranco

MILLER BAJO

C. Carmen

C. Pino

Calle Diego

Vega

Sarmiento

H

Víctor Pérez Calle

Camino

Andenes

Fusta

Mazurca

C.

Calle

Rancho de Ánimas

Malaguenas

Farias

Fama

Fragua

C.

C.

Viejo

Zorondongo

Polca

Tajaraste

Isas

Arrorro

de

Guiniguada

Cuevas de Niz

F

Quintana

Apolinario

C.

Eufemiano

Navarro

Fuentes

Cabrera

Sánchez

Camino Galo o Viera

I

MILLER ALTO

Alfredo M. Reyes

C

Pasa a pág. 17.

Pasa a pág. 24.

Estación Depuradora

C. Thomas Mann

Batán

C. Robert Koch

C.

Secadero

Polvorín

La Providencia

Km. 1

EL BATAN

Urbanización El Batán

Albert

Gabriela

George Prie

Schweitzer

C. Marie

C. Yanusari

Curie

Luigi Prandello

Kawata

M. Angel Asturias

Calle

Alexis

Bernard Shaw

Mistral

Rabindranath Tagore

Rudyard Kipling

C. Carlos S. Lamas

M. Lutero King

Severo Ochoa

A

B

C

Seguidillas

C. Tafira

Ernest

Carrel

Hemingway

Temple

Arrorro

Plaza Ntra. Sra. de Fátima

C. Siriroque

Saltonas

C. Párroco Segundo Vega

Masequera

Barranco

Camino

Barahona

D

E

F

de

Lugarejo

Guiniguada

C. Pino

LOMO BLANCO

Apolinario

Plaza Obispo Marquina

Bienvenido Pampliega

P. G. Pascual

G

H

I

P. Villafán

Ana Benitez

C. González Guedes

LOMO APOLINARIO

Pasa a pág. 25.

Viene de pág. 16.

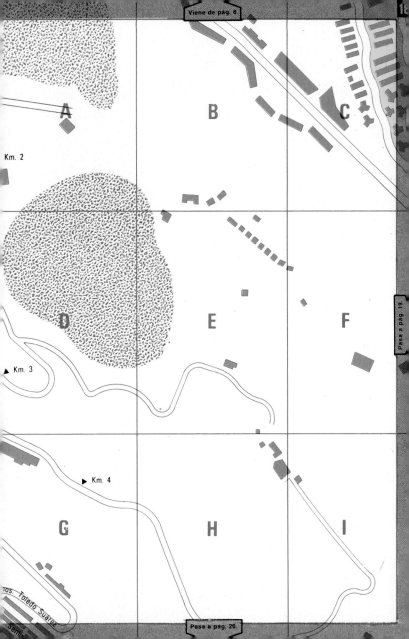

A

Km. 2

B

C

D

E

F

Pasa a pág. 19

Km. 3

Km. 4

G

H

I

ros. Toledo Suárez

Santa

Pasa a pág. 26.

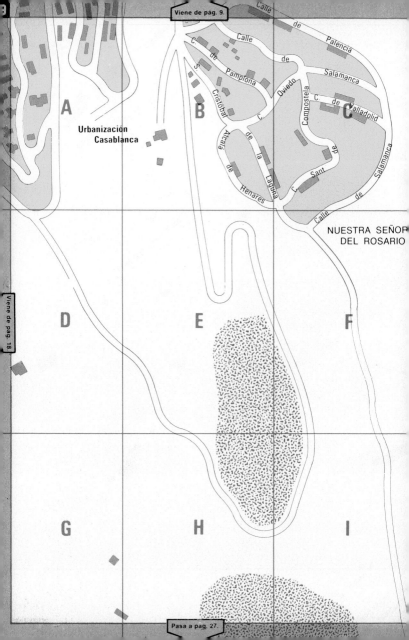

Viene de pág. 9.

Viene de pág. 18

Calle
Calle de Palencia
Calle de Pamplona
de
Oviedo
de Salamanca
C. de Valladolid
Compostela
C.
S. Cristóbal
Alcalá
de la Laguna
C.
C.
Henares
C. Sant
de Salamanca
de

Calle

A

Urbanización
Casablanca

B

C

NUESTRA SEÑORA
DEL ROSARIO

D

E

F

G

H

I

Pasa a pág. 27.

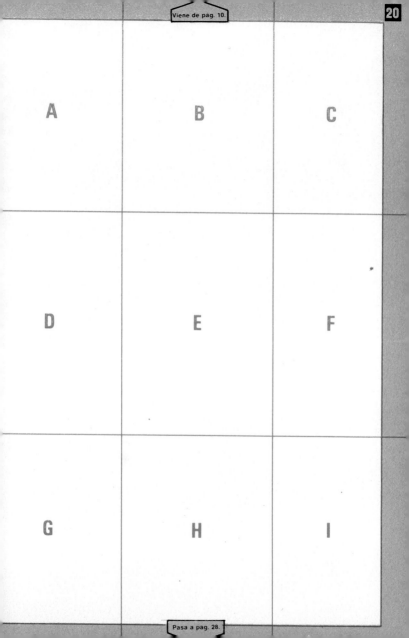

A

B

C

D

E

F

G

H

I

Pasa a pag. 28.

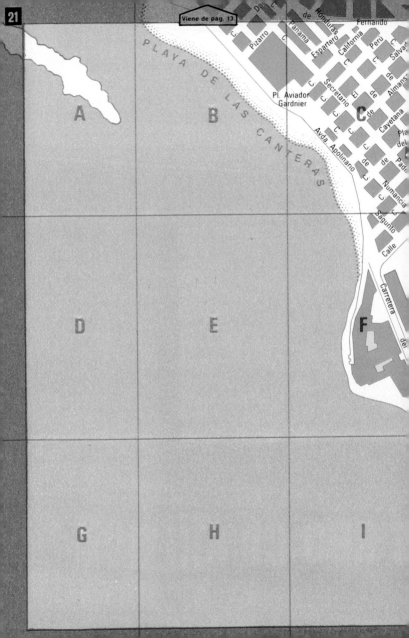

21

Viene de pag. 13.

A

PLAYA DE LAS CANTERAS

B

Dai. C.
de
Honduras
Panamá
Fernando
C.
Pizarro
Espartero
California
Perú
C.
Salvar
de
Secretario
El
de
Almans
Pl. Aviador
Gardnier
C.
C.
C.
C.
C.
Cayetana
C.
Avda. Apolinario
Pla
del
Pad
de
de
C.
Numancia
C.
C.
C.
Sagunto

C

Calle

D

E

Carretera

F

Carretera del

G

H

I

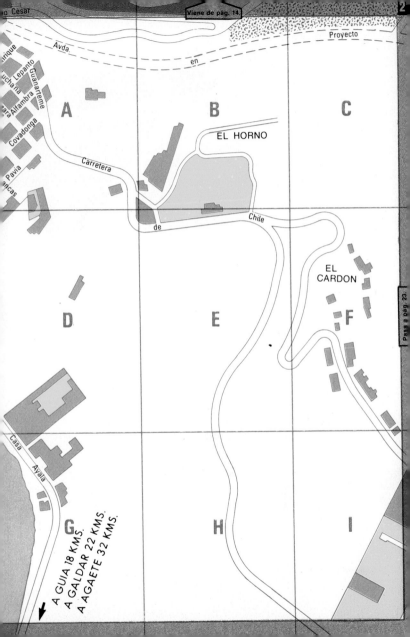

Pasa a pág. 23.

o Cesar

Avda

Proyecto

en

rique
Lepanto
Guanarteme
ucha na
Alfambra
a
Covadonga

Pavia

ancas

A

B

C

EL HORNO

Carretera

de   Chile

EL
CARDON

D

E

F

Casa

Ayala

G

H

I

A GUIA 18 KMS.
A GALDAR 22 KMS.
A AGAETE 32 KMS.

Viene de pág. 15.

Viene de pág. 22

Avda.

en

Proyecto

A

B

Calle

C. de

Pacuco Penichet

Guillermo

Santana

Diego   Betancurt

Provisional

Suárez

C

Sargento

Alférez   Provisional

Calle

D

E

F

LAS TORRES
BAJAS

LAS TORRES ALTAS

Carretera

de

Tamaraceite

G

H

I

DIAZ CASANOVA

Urbanización Industrial

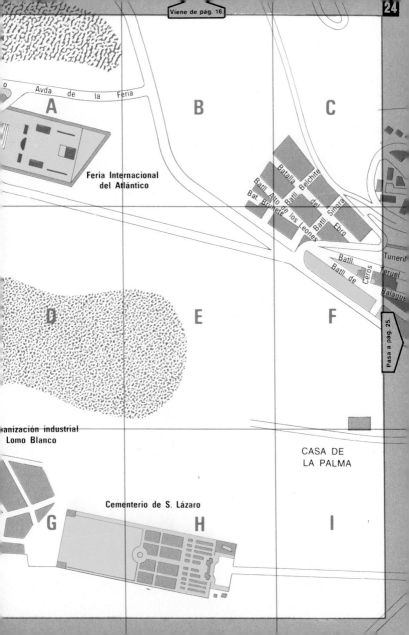

Avda. de la Feria

A

B

C

Feria Internacional
del Atlántico

Batalla Belchite

Batll. Alto Batll. del

Batll. de los Leones

Bat. Brunete

Batll. Singra

Batll. Ebro

Batll. Tuneril

Batll. de Ceros

Teruel

Balague

D

E

F

Pasa a pág. 25.

anización industrial
Lomo Blanco

CASA DE
LA PALMA

Cementerio de S. Lázaro

G

H

I

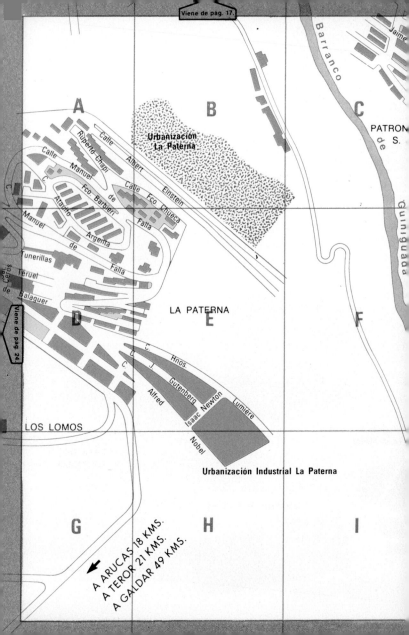

Viene de pág. 17.

Viene de pág. 24

A

B

Urbanización
La Paterna

C

PATRON
S.

Calle Ruperto Chapí

Calle Albert Einstein

Calle

Manuel de

Fco Barbieri

Calle Fco Chueca

Atarnio

Argenta

Falla

de

Manuel

de

Falla

Tunerillas

Teruel

Balaguer

D

E

LA PATERNA

F

Barranco

Guiniguada

Jaime

C. J. Hnos.

Gutenberg

Alfred

Isaac Newton

Lumiere

Nobel

Urbanización Industrial La Paterna

LOS LOMOS

G

H

I

A ARUCAS 18 KMS.
A TEROR 21 KMS.
A GALDAR 49 KMS.

Viene de pág. 18.

Toledo Suárez
Seminario
rtel

Km. 5 ◄

PICO VIENTO

A

B

C

SANO

EL PILAR

Pasa a pág. 27.

HUESAS

ZURBARAN

OREGAL **D**

E

F

Urbanización Zurbarán

CORONEL PERERA

G Barranco del Colegio

H

I

FUENTE MORALES

Viene de pág. 19.

Colegio Sagrado Corazón

A

B

C

Km. 6 ▼

Patagonia

Sta. Fe

Formosa

C.

Salta C.

Bruno

Naranjo

Tucumán

Pampa

MEDIO PAÑUELO

Viene de pág. 26.

D

E

F

Km. 7 ▼

QUILMES

TAFIRA BAJA

Urbanización Cruz Queved

G

H

I

Km. 8 ◄

Viene de pág. 20.

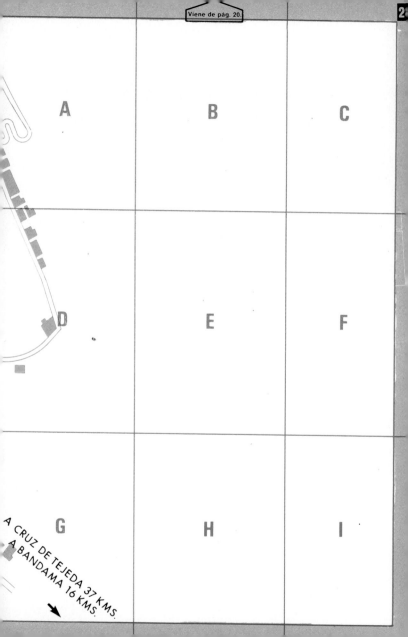

A

B

C

D

E

F

G

H

I

A CRUZ DE TEJEDA 37 KMS.
A BANDAMA 16 KMS.

CALLEJERO DE LAS PALMAS DE GRAN CANARIA

INDICE ALFABETICO

CALLE / RUE / STREET / STRASSE	PLANO / CLEF / KEY / SCHLÜSSEL	CALLE / RUE / STREET / STRASSE	PLANO / CLEF / KEY / SCHLÜSSEL
Bruno Naranjo	27.E	Ctra. a el Lasso	8.F-I
Buenos Aires	5.F-6.D	Ctra. de Chile	22.A-C
		Ctra. del Rincón a Casa Ayala	21.F-22.G
		Ctra. de Tamaraceite	23.G-H
		Ctra. de Mata	6.G
C		Ctra. del Norte	16.A-D-H
Cactus (B.º de S. José).		Carrillo (B.º de S. José).	
Cadena	7.I	Carvajal	5.G
Cádiz	15.C	Casandra	5.I
Cairasco (Pl.)	6.E	Cascabel (B.º de S. José).	
Cal	6.F	Castaño	7.G
Calesa (B.º de S. José).		Castillejos	21.C
Caleta	12.D	Castillo	6.F
Califa	7.I	Castor Gómez Navarro	16.H-I
California	21.C	Castrillo	5.G
Calvo Sotelo	6.E	Cayetano Manrique	21.C-22.A
Callejón del Molino	6.H	Cebrián	5.F
Cambaluz	1.I	Celia	16.G
Camilo Saint Saëns	14.D	Celta	7.E
Camino	17.E	Ceniza (B.º de S. José).	
Camino Galo o Viera	16.I	Centella	7.D
Camino Viejo de Tafira	16.C	Cepillo (B.º de S. José).	
	17.A	Ceres	24.F
Camino al Polvorín	17.B	Cerezo	7.E
	7.G-H	Cerrojo	7.E
Campana (B.º de S. José).		Cirilo Moreno	13.D
Campoamor	14.D	Ciruelo	7.G
Canal (B.º de S. José).		Clarín	7.E
Canalejas	5.H-F	Clavel	6.D
Candado	7.H	Cobre	7.H
Candelaria de León	9.H	Codo	7.E
Candil	6.F	Colacho Massieu (Pl.)	14.H-I
Cano	6.D	Colmenares	5.F
Cantabria (B.º de S. José).		Colombia	13.H
Canteras (Paseo de las)	12.D-F	Colón	6.E
	13.G-H	Cte. Ramón Franco (Pl.)	12.F
Cañada (B.º de S. José).		Cometa	7.H
Capa (B.º de S. José).		Comino (B.º de S. José)	
Cptán. Eliseo L. Orduña	15.B	Compás	7.E
Capitán Lucena	12.F	Concepción Arenal	13.E-F
Caracas	13.I	Concha Espina	6.E
Caracol (B.º de S. José).		Conde de Albrit	5.I
Cardo	7.D	Condesa de Lain	5.I-6.G
Carlos M. Blandy	15.D	Constantino	6.D
Carlos de S. Lamas	17.F	Coral	7.D
Carmelo Bethencourt	15.C	Corbeta	7.E
Carmen Quintana	16.E-F	Córdoba	7.D-F
Carmín (B.º de S. José).		Cornisa (Paseo de la)	14.E
Ctra del Centro	6.I-7.G	Corona	7.E

CALLE RUE STREET STRASSE	PLANO CLEF KEY SCHLÜSSEL	CALLE RUE STREET STRASSE	PLANO CLEF KEY SCHLÜSSEL
Coronel Rocha	11.B-E 1.H	Dr. Centeno	15.C
		Dr. Deniz	6.E
Corregidor Aguirre	6.F	Dr. Chil	6.B-E
Corsario	7.E	Dr. Eustasio Quevedo	15.D
Costa Rica	13.I	Dr. Fleming	14.F
Covadonga	21.C-22.A	Dr. Gómez-Ulla	15.D
Cruce de S. Juan (B.º de S.Juan)		Dr. Grau Bassas	12.F-13.D
Cruz de Piedra	16.B-E	Dr. J. León Molaces	15.G
Cuarenta Casas	13.H	Dr. Jiménez Neyra	15.C
Cuatro Cañones	15.A	Dr. Juan de Padilla	6.D
Curva	15.B	Dr. Marañón	16.G-H
Cuevas de Niz	16.F	Dr. Manuel de la Nuez	6.E
		Dr. Miguel Rosa	12.F
		Dr. Nuez Aguilar	6.F
CH		Dr. Rafael González	6.D
		Dr. Raf. O'sanahan (Pl.)	4.I
Chapas	5.G	Dr. Sventennius	
Chasuas Sicilia	15.G	Dr. Ventura Ramirez	6.F
Chil (Paseo del)	5.I 13.F-D 14.E-C 15.A-B	Dr. Verneau	6.F
		Dr. Waksman	5.H
		Dr. Woelfel	14.F
		Dolores de la Rocha	6.C
Chopin	14.F	Dolly	5.I
Churruca	13.H	Domingo Déniz	5.E
		Domingo Doreste	6.C
		Dgo. Guerra del Rio	6.E-G
D		Domingo J. Navarro	6.D
		Domingo Padrón	16.G
Dalia	7.I	Domingo Rivero	14.C
Daoiz	21.B 13.H-I	Don Benito (Pl.)	15.B
		Doñana (B.º de S. José).	
Deán López Martin	16.A	Doña Perfecta	15.F
Dean Rodriguez Bolaños	15.H	Doramas (Pl.)	15.H
De Bussy	9.D-G	Doramas	6.E
De los Balcanes	6.E	Doramas (Parque)	14.B-C
Delicia	7.I	Dos de Mayo	13.G
Delfin (B.º de S. José).		Dragón	7.H
Demetria	5.I	Duero	7.I
Déniz	6.B	Dulcenombre	6.G
Diana	7.I	Dvòřak	9.D
Diderot	13.E		
Diego A. Montaude	6.C		
Diego B. Suárez	2;.C	**E**	
Diego Miguel	14.F		
Diego de Ordaz	12.E	Ebro	7.H
Diego Vega Sarmiento	16.E-I	Eco	7.H
Diego Zorita	15.D	Echegaray	15.D-E
Dr. Apolinario Macias	14.E	Eduardo	5.F
Dr. C. Quevedo	15.G	Eduardo Benitez González	15.E
		Eduardo Benot	12.E-F

CALLE / RUE / STREET / STRASSE	PLANO / CLEF / KEY / SCHLÜSSEL	CALLE / RUE / STREET / STRASSE	PLANO / CLEF / KEY / SCHLÜSSEL
Fresa	6.I	Gerona	15.C
Fresno	7.G	Giralda (B.º de S. Nicolas).	
Frías	6.E	Girasol	6.E
Fuente	6.E	Globo	6.E
Fuerteventura	12.E	Gloria	5.I
Funchal	12.D-E	Golfo	6.E
Fusta	16.C	Gomera	12.E
		Gómez Escuderos	15.D-G
		Góngora	14.E
		González Guedes	17.G
G		Gordillo	11.C-12.A
		Graciliano Alfonso	14.A
Gabarra	6.E	Granate	6.H
Gabriel Araceli	5.I	Granadera Canaria	7.A-D
Gabriel Miró	14.E	Gran Canaria	12.A-D
Gabriela Mistral	17.B	Gravina	13.H
Gabriel Mejias	16.H	Gregorio Gutiérrez (B.º de S. Nicolas).	
Gabriel y Galán	7.I	Guadarfía	11.B
Gacela	6.H	Guadiana	6.H
Gago Goutinho	14.B	Guanchía	11.B
Galera	6.H	Guanhaben	1.I
Galgo	6.H	Guatemala	13.H
Galicia	13.E	Guayadeque	11.E
Galileo	13.G-E	Guayedra	11.C
Galo Ponte	5.H	Guayres	11.C
Galón	6.E	Guillermo Santana Rivero	23.B-24.A
Gamonal	11.F	Gunidafe	11.C
García Castrillo, Dr.	14.E	Gustavo J. N. Nieto	15.H-I
García del Castillo	14.E-F		
García Morato	14.E		
García Tello	6.F	**H**	
Garita	11.F		
Gato (B.º de S. Nicolas).		Habana	13.I
Gaviota (B.º de S. Nicoláy).		Halma	15.C
General	8.E	Harimaguadas	1.I
General Balmes	12.B-C	Henry Dunant	15.E-I
General Bravo	6.D	Hnos. García de la Torre	14.D
General Goded	14.A	Hnos. Jorge Marrero	11.E
General Martínez Anido	5.H	Hnos. Lumière	25.E
General Más de Gaminde	13.E-F	Hnos. Millares (Parque)	15.G
General Orgaz	11.F-12.D	Hnos. Toledo Suárez	18.G-26.A
General Prim (Pl.)	15.C	Hermosilla, Regente	15.B
General Sanjurjo	13.G-H	Hernán Cortés (Pl.)	13.D
General Vives	1;.D-E	Hernán Pérez	6.F
	12.F	Héroes del Alcázar (Pl.)	5.H
George Bernard Shaw	17.B	Herrería	6.E
George Pire	17.B	Hierro (Isla de)	12.E
Geranio (B.º de S. José).		Honduras	21.C

CALLE / RUE / STREET / STRASSE	PLANO / CLEF / KEY / SCHLÜSSEL	CALLE / RUE / STREET / STRASSE	PLANO / CLEF / KEY / SCHLÜSSEL
Matula	6.D	Ntra. Sra. de los Dolores (Plaza)	15.F
Máximo	16.G	Ntra. Sra. de Fátima (Plaza)	17.A
Mayor de Triana	5.F-6.D	Ntra. Sra. de la Paz	16.D
Mayorazgo	11.F	Ntra. Sra. del Pino (Plaza)	5.I-6.G
Mazurca	16.C	Ntra. Sra. de los Reyes (Plaza)	7.D
Mediodía (B.º de S. José)		Numancia	21.C
Menceyes	1.I-11.C	Núñez de Arce	14.B
Mendizábal	6.B	Núñez de Balboa	15.B-E
Menéndez y Pelayo	13.E-F	Núñez de la Peña	5.I
Mercado (Pl.)	6.B		
Mercurio (B.º de S. Nicolás)	6.D		
Mesa de León (Fco.)	6.E	**O**	
Miguel AngelhAsturias	17.A-B		
Miguel Benitez Inglott	14.D-I	Obispo Albiturria	9.I
Miguel Gil	9.B	Obispo Codina	6.E
Miguel Sarmiento	14.C	Obispo Frias (Pl.)	15.E-H
Miguel Servet	7.D	Obispo Encina	5.H-15.B
Milagro	6.E	Obispo Herrera	1;.D
Milanera (Pl.)	13.I	Obispo Marquina (Pl.)	17.H
Milton (Pl.)	14.D	Obispo Romo	15.E
Minerva	6.D	Obispo Servera	15.F
Minilla, La	13.H	Obispo Serra Sucarrats	15.H
Minindra	6.D	Obispo Tavira	14.F
Mirasol (B.º de S. Nicolás)		Obispo Urquinaona	14.F
Misericordia	16.G	Obispo Vela	15.A
Mister Blisse	6.E	Oceanía	7.E
Molino de Viento	5.G-H	Oñate	16.G
Moneda (B.º de S. Nicolás)	6.E	Ortiz de Zárate	14.F-15.D
Monsalud	15.B	Osorio	11.C
Montes de Oca	6.B	Oviedo	19.B-C
Montevideo	13.D		
Moratin	15.Z	**P**	
Mozart	14.D		
Munguia	6.D	P. G. Pascual	17.G
Murga	5.E-I	Pablo Penáguilas	15.F
Muro	6.E	Pacuco Penichet	23.B
		Padre Anchieta	14.F
N		Padre Claret	15.B
		Padre Cueto	12.E
Navarro Ruiz	14.E	Padre Hilario (Pl.)	5.F
Navarro Torrent	15.H	Padre José de Sosa	6.C
Navidad (Pl. de la)	16.D	Padre Raymond	13.D
Nazarin (B.º de S. Nicolás)		Padre Serna	15.H
Nelly	5.I-6.G	Padre Villalain	17.G
Néstor (Glorieta)	14.C	Pajonales	12.D
Néstor de la Torre	13.E	Palafox	13.H-I
Nicolás Estévanez	12.F	Palencia	9.H-I
Nieve	6.E		19.C
Nilo (B.4 de S. Nicolás)	6.E	Palma de Mallorca	7.E
Nogal	6.D	Palmar	1.I-11.C

DIRECCIONES DE URGENCIA DE LAS PALMAS DE GRAN CANARIA

Bomberos	Plaza Tomás Morales	Telf. 243100
Casa de Socorro de Las Palmas	Plaza Tomás Morales	Telf. 245157
Casa de Socorro del Puerto	Albareda, 198	Telf. 264473
Clínica de Urgencia	León y Castillo, 66	Telf. 220500
Clínica British American	Núñez de Arce, 2	Telf. 245876
Clínica Cajal	Senador Castillo Olivares	Telf. 217700
Clínica de la Casa del Marino	Edf. de la Casa del Marino	Telf. 260670
Clínica Nuestra Sra. de La Paloma	Maestro Valle, 18	Telf. 242948
Clínica Oftalmológica	Perdomo, 45	Telf. 221610
Clínica San José	Padre Cueto, 28	Telf. 263720
Clínica San Roque	D. de La Rocha, 5	Telf. 223640
Clínica Sta. Catalina	León y Castillo, 364	Telf. 243940
Cruz Roja Española	León y Castillo, 243	Telf. 245921
Gas Butano	Tomás Morales, 20	Telf. 220902
Guardia Civil	Agustín Millares, 17	Telf. 215758
Guardia Municipal	Obispo Frías, 1	Telf. 253998
Hospital Inglés	P.º de la Cornisa	Telf. 254243
Policía (comisaria)	Plaza La Feria	Telf. 215817
Servicio de Abastecimiento de Aguas	San Juan, s/n.	Telf. 219567
Unión Eléctrica de Canarias	S. Bernardo, 3	Telf. 221543

DISTANCIAS KILOMETRICAS DESDE LAS PALMAS A:

NORTE		SUR		CENTRO	
Kms.		Kms.		Kms.	
7	Tamaraceite	13	Teide	8	Tafira
17	Arucas	18	Gando (Aeropuerto)	10	Monte Coello
25	Firgas	22	Valsequillo	14	Santa Brígida
30	Moya	27	Ingenio	21	San Mateo
38	Jardin de Corvo	29	Agüimes	21	Teror
42	Fontanales	47	Sta. Lucía de T.	29	Valleseco
37	Sta. María de Guía	54	San Bartolomé de T.	35	Cruz de Tejeda
40	Gáldar	65	Fataga	44	Tejeda
49	Agaete	36	Cruce de Sardina	46	Artenara
57	Los Berrazales	44	San Agustin	51	Tamadaba
84	San Nicolás de T.	58	Maspalomas		
		64	Arguineguin		
		66	Patalavaca		
		68	Puerto Rico		
		86	Mogán		

CLIMATOLOGIA DE GRAN CANARIA. CLIMATOLOGIE DE GRANDE CANARIE. CLIMATOLOGY OF GRAN CANARIA. KLIMATABELLE VON GRAN CANARIA. GRAN CANARIAS KLIMAT

TEMPERATURA CELSIUS				PRESION ATMOSFERICA 1		HUMEDAD 2	LLUVIA 3	INSOLACION 4
	5 máxima	6 media	7 minima	5 máxima	7 minima	8 relativa media %	9 litros m²	%
Enero	22,8	17,4	12,1	765,8	762,9	73	31,7	57
Febrero	23,1	17,4	11,9	764,8	763,4	72	29,4	59
Marzo	24,3	17,6	12,4	763,5	760,5	71	3,7	61
Abril	24,0	18,3	13,0	762,7	759,9	71	4,8	57
Mayo	25,4	19,9	25,0	762,6	760,4	70	2,4	61
Junio	34,3	21,0	17,7	762,7	760,9	70	0,0	65
Julio	36,9	22,1	18,3	762,2	760,0	66	0,0	65
Agosto	39,7	23,7	29,6	771,2	759,9	71	0,0	70
Septiembre	29,5	23,6	19,1	762,1	759,8	74	4,4	60
Octubre	28,2	22,4	16,2	762,7	760,5	74	25,9	64
Noviembre	26,9	20,6	15,0	762,8	760,1	71	42,4	57
Diciembre	24,5	18,6	12,6	765,2	762,6	72	43,6	59

1) Pression atmosphérique, atmospheric pressure, atmosphärischer Druck. Lufttryck.
2) Humidité, humidity, Luftfeuchtigkeit, fuktighet.
3) Pluie, rainfall, Niederschlage, regn.
4) Insolation, insolation, Sonnenschein, soldagar.
5) Maximum, maximum, Höchstw, max.
6) Moyenne, average, Mittelw, medeltal.
7) Minimum, minimum, Mindestw, min.
8) Relative moyenne %, relative average %, relative Mittelwert, medeltal %.
9) Litres par m², liters per m², Liter pro m², per m.

INFORMACIÓN PRÁCTICA
LAS PALMAS-LANZAROTE-FUERTEVENTURA

INFORMATION PRATIQUE
LAS PALMAS-LANZAROTE-FUERTEVENTURA

PRACTICAL INFORMATION
LAS PALMAS-LANZAROTE-FUERTEVENTURA

PRAKTISCHE HINWELSE
LAS PALMAS-LANZAROTE-FUERTEVENTURA

PRACKTISKA UPPLYSNINGAR OM
LAS PALMAS-LANZAROTE-FUERTEVENTURA

Para cualquier otra información, puede Vd. dirigirse a la Oficina de Turismo, sita en: Parque de Santa Catalina. Las Palmas de Gran Canaria. Parque Municipal. Arrecife de Lanzarote. Parador Nacional de Turismo. Puerto del Rosario (Fuerteventura).

Pour toute information, vous pouvez vous adresser au Bureau du Tourisme, situé: Parque de Santa Catalina. Las Palmas de Gran Canaria. Parque Municipal. Arrecife de Lanzarote. Parador Nacional de Turismo. Puerto del Rosario (Fuerteventura).

For further information, visit the Tourist Office, located at: Parque de Santa Catalina. Las Palmas de Gran Canaria. Parque Municipal. Arrecife de Lanzarote. Parador Nacional de Turismo. Puerto del Rosario (Fuerteventura).

Zur Erhaltung irgendeiner anderen Auskunft können Sie sich an das Turismusbüro in der Parque de Santa Catalina. Las Palmas de Gran Canaria. Parque Municipal. Arrecife de Lanzarote. Parador Nacional de Turismo. Puerto del Rosario (Fuerteventura).

Vidare upplysningar erhälles vid hänvändelse till Turistbyrån (Oficina de Turismo) i, adress: Parque de Santa Catalina. Las Palmas de Gran Canaria. Parque Municipal. Arrecife de Lanzarote. Parador Nacional de Turismo. Puerto del Rosario (Fuerteventura).

1. ARTE Y CULTURA
ART ET CULTURE
ART AND CULTURE
KUNST UND KULTUR
KONST OCH KULTUR

1.1. CONJUNTO MONUMENTAL
ENSEMBLE MONUMENTAL
MONUMENTS
SEHENSWURDIGKEITEN
BYGGNADER AV HISTORISK-ARKITEKTONISKT INTRESSE SAMT MONUMENT

Las Palmas

CATEDRAL. *CATHÉDRALE.*
CATHEDRAL. *KATHEDRALE.*
KATEDRALEN.

Comenzada a construir en 1497, de estilo gótico, contiene un rico tesoro de ornamentos litúrgicos y de cuadros. En ella se custodia el Pendón de la Conquista. Entre sus obras más valiosas figura un portapaz, obra de Benvenuto Cellini, así como varias imágenes talladas por el escultor canario Luján Pérez, un cuadro del pintor Roelas y otro del Divino Morales.

On commença sa construction en 1497 en style gothique et elle garde un riche trésor en ornements liturgiques et en tableaux. On y garde l'Étendard de la Conquête. Parmi les plus précieuses oeuvres d'art figure une patène due à Benvenuto Cellini, ainsi que quelques sculptures taillées par l'artiste canarien Luján Pérez, un tableau du peintre Roelas et un autre de Morales.

Its construction was initiated in 1497. It has a Gothic style and contains a rich treasure of liturgic ornaments and paintings. The Standard of the Conquest is kept here. Among its most valuable works is a pix of Benvenuto Cellini, and various engraved statues by the Canary sculptor Luján Pérez, a painting by the Painter Roelas, and one by the Divine Morales.

Gotischer Bau, 1497 begonnén, mit wertuoller Schatzsammlung liturgischer Gewänder und Bilder. Aufbewahrungsort der Wiedereroberungsstandarte. Zu den wertvollsten Werken gehört ein Portapaz von Benvenuto Cellini, sowie verschiedene vom kanarischen Bildhauer Luján Pérez gefertigte Statuen, ein Bild des Malers Roelas und ein wei eres von Divino Morales.

Denna, uppförd i gotisk stil, påbörjades år 1497. Den äger en rik skatt avaltarprydnader och tavlor. Här förvaras fanan som de spanska erövrarna bar. Bland de värdefullaste föremålen kan nämnas en fridsbringare av Benvenuto Cellini samt flera helgonfigurer snidade av den lokale skulptören Luján Pérez, en tavla av målaren Roelas och en annan av Morales.

ERMITA DE SAN ANTONIO ABAD
ERMITAGE DE SAINT ANTOINE ABBÉ (San Antonio Abad)
HERMITAGE OF ST. ANTHONY ABAD
KAPELLE DES ABTES SAN ANTONIO
KAPELLET SAN ANTONIO ABAD

Plaza de San Antonio Abad. Obra del siglo XVII levantada en el solar del templo en que estuvo situada la iglesia en la cual, según tradición, oró Cirstóbal Colón en el viaje del Descubrimiento.

*Plaza de San Antonio Abad. Oeuvre du XVII*s. érigé sur le terrain du temple où se trouvait située l'église dans laquelle, selon la tradition, Christophe Colomb pria lors du voyage de la Découverte.*

Plaza de San Antonio Abad. A work of the XVII century which was built on the lot where, according to tradition, the church was located in which Christopher Columbus prayed on his way to Discover America.

Plaza de San Antonio Abad. Bau aus dem 17. jahrhundert, auf dem selben Grundstück errichtet auf dem früher die Kirche stand in der, laut Überlieferung, Christoph Kolumbus auf seiner Entdeckungsreise betete.

Plaza de San Antonio Abad. Kapellet uppbyggd på platsen var den kyrka låg var Kolumbus bad under sin upptäcksfärd, detta efter traditionssägen.

CEMENTERIO VIEJO
VIEUX CIMETIÈRE
OLD CEMENTERY
ALTER FRIEDHOF
GAMLA KYRKOGÅRDEN

Avenida Marítima del Sur. Puede admirarse en él la tumba del poeta Tomás Morales, obra de Victorio Macho.

Avda. Marítima del Sur. On peut y admirer la tombe du poète Tomás Morales, oeuvre de Victorio Macho.

Avda. Marítima del Sur. Here one can admire the tomb of the poet Tomás Morales, a work by Victorio Macho.

Avenida Marítima del Sur. Dort befindet sich das Grabmal des Dichters Tomás Morales, das ein Werk von Victorio Macho ist.

Avenida Marítima del Sur. På denna kyrkogård kan man beundra poeten Tomás Morales grav, verk av Victorio Macho.

BARRIO DE VEGUETA
BARRIO DE VEGUETA
VEGUETA SECTOR
VEGUETA-VIERTEL
VEGUETAS STADSDEL

Se trata del barrio más antiguo de la ciudad, notable por el carácter de sus edificios, en los que la arquitectura colonial hispánica da sus primeros vagidos.

It s'agit du quartier le plus ancien de la ville, remarquable pour le caractère de ses édifices, où l'architecture coloniale hispanique fit ses premiers pas.

This is the oldest neighborhood of the city, notable for the nature of its buildings which show signs of the Hispanic colonial architectural style.

Es handelt sich hier um das äteste Viertel der Stadt; seine Gebäude sind besonders interessant, da man hier die Anfänge der spanischen Kolonialarchitektur beobachten kann.

Denna stadsdel är den äldsta och nämnvärd för dess typiska byggnader i vilka man märker den första stöten, med tanke på arkitekturen, mot den spanska kolonialstilen.

CASTILLO DE LA LUZ
CHÂTEAU DE LA LUZ
CASTLE OF LIGHT
LICHTERSCHLOSS
CASTILLO DE LA LUZ

Bastión de la resistencia canaria contra los ataques de los piratas en el siglo XVI. Está situado al fondo de la antigua dársena y ha sido declarado Monumento Histórico.

Bastion de la résistance canarienne contre les attaques des pirates du XVIème siècle. Il se trouve au fond du vieil arrière-port et il a été déclaré Monument Historique.

The Canary bastion of resistence against the pirate attacks of the XVI century. It lies at the bottom of the ancient dock and has been declared a Historic Monument.

Bollwerk des kanarischen Widerstands gegen Angriffe der Piraten im XVI Jahrhundert. Es liegt am Ende des alten Hafenbeckens und wird als historisches. Denkmal bezeichnet.

Här försvarade sig öborna mot sjörövare under 1500-talet. Fortet är beläget längst inne i den gamla hamnen, och har blivit officiellt förklarat historiskt minnesmärke.

Lanzarote

CASTILLO DE SAN GABRIEL
CHÂTEAU DE SAINT GABRIEL
CASTLE OF SAINT GABRIEL
SCHLOSS DES HL. GABRIELS
CASTILLO DE SAN GABRIEL

Se levanta en un islote frente al casco de la ciudad, reconstruido en 1590 por Torriani para defender Arrecife contra los continuos ataques de los piratas berberiscos. Está unido a la ciudad por un puente levadizo, llamado de «Las Bolas», y jugó su papel en las aventuras y piraterías de los siglos XV, XVI y XVII.

Il s'élève sur un îlot, face à la ville, reconstruit en 1590 par Torriani, pour défendre Arrecife contre les continuels attaques des pirates mauresques. Il est uni à la ville par un pont-levis, appelé de «Las Bolas» (Les Boules), et il eut son rôle dans les aventures et les pirateries des XVème, XVIème et XVIIème siècles.

This is built on an small island facing the town centre and was rebuilt in 1590 by Torriani to protect Arrecife against the continuous attacks by the Berber pirates. It is joined to the town by a lifting bridge called «Las Bolas» and played its part in the adventures and piracys of the XV, XVI and XVII centuries.

Es erhebt sich auf einem Eiland dem Stadtkern gegenüber. 1590 wurde es wiedererbaut zum Schutze von Arrecife gegen die ständigen. Angriffe der Berberpiraten. Eine Zugbrücke «Las Bolas» verbindet das Schloss mit der Stadt; sie spielte eine wichtige Rolle bei den abenteuerlichen Seeräuberüberfällen in XV XVI und XVII. Jahrhundert.

Denna fästning, som reser sig på en holme utanför staden, återuppbyggdes 1590 av Torriani för att försvara Arrecife mot de nordafrikanska piraternas ständiga anfall. Det är förenat med staden genom en vindbrygga kallad «Las Bolas», och spelade en viktig roll under sjöröveriets och äventyrens tid på 1400-, 1500- och 1600-talen.

CASTILLO DE SAN JOSÉ
CHÂTEAU DE SAN JOSEPH
CASTLE OF SAINT JOSEPH
SCHLOSS DES HL. JOSEPH
CASTILLO DE SAN JOSÉ

Construido en el año 1779 por orden del rey Carlos III. También es digna de ser visitada la iglesia parroquial de San Ginés, patrona de la Isla.

Construit dans l'année 1779, sur l'ordre du Roi Charles III. L'église paroissiale de San Ginés, Patron de l'Ile, est aussi digne d'être visitée.

Built in 1779 by order of King Charles III. The Parish church of Saint Ginés, the Island's Patron Saint, also deserves a visit.

1779 auf Geheiss König Karl III erbaut. Besuchenswert ist auch die Pfarrkirche der Hl. Ginés, der Inselpatronin.

Uppfört år 1779 på order av kung Carlos III. San Ginés församlingskyrka är även värd ett besök.

Fuerteventura

CASA DE LOS CORONELES
MAISON DES COLONELS
HOUSE OF THE COLONELS
HAUS DER OBERSTEN
CASA DE LOS CORONELES

En la Oliva y entre sus viejos edificios se encuentra esta Casa, considerada como la más representativa construcción del siglo XVIII en el archipiélago.

Dans La Oliva, et parmi ses vieux édifices, on trouve cette Maison considerée comme la construction la plus représentative du XVIIIème siècle dans l'archipel.

In the village of Oliva, and amid its old buildings one con find this House which is considered as the best representative construction of the XVIII century in the Archipelago.

Das Haus befindet sich in La Oliva, umgeben von dessen alten Gebäuden. Allgemein betrachtet man es als das representativste Gebaäude aus dem XVIII Jahrhundert auf dem Archipel.

«Överstarnas hus» ligger bland de gamla byggnaderna i la Oliva och anses vara den byggning som bäst representerar öarnas 1700-talsarkitektur.

1.2. MUSEOS
MUSEÉS
MUSEUMS
MUSEUM
MUSEER

Las Palmas

MUSEO PROVINCIAL DE BELLAS ARTES
MUSÉE PROVINCIAL DE BEAUX-ARTS
PROVINCIAL MUSEUM OF FINE ARTS
LANDESMUSEUM DER SCHÖNEN KÜNSTE
PROVINSMUSEET «BELLAS ARTES»

Instalado en el mismo edificio de la Casa de Colón. En él puede admirarse obras de los más importantes artistas canarios, así como tambien lienzos y esculturas de célebres maestros españoles, sobre todo contemporáneos, tales como Regoyos, Solana, Manolo Hugué, etc.

Installé dans l'édifice mème de la Casa de Colón. On peut y admirer des oeuvres des plus importants artistes canariens, ainsi que des tableaux et des sculptures de célèbres maîtres espagnols, surtout contemporains, tels que Regoyos, Solana, Manolo Hugué, etc.

Installed in the same building as the House of Columbus. One can admire works by the most important artists of the Canary Islands, as well as canvases and sculptures by famous Spanish masters, especially contemporary ones such as Regoyos, Solana, Manolo Hugué, etc.

Befindet sich in dem selben Gebäude wie das Haus des Kolumbus. Dort kann man die bedeutendsten Werke kanarischer Künstler bewundern und es befinden sich dort auch Ölgemälde und Skulpturen von berühmten spanischen Meistern, vor allem von zeitgenössischen, wie Regoyos, Solana, Manolo Hugué, u. a.

Installerat i själva Casa de Colón. I deffa museum kan man beundra konstverk av de mest framstaende kanariska konstnärer även väggmälningar och skulpturer av kända spanska mästare. Men framförallt, de nutida såsom Regoyos, Solana, Manolo Hugué, o.s.v.

MUSEO CANARIO
MUSÉE CANARIEN
CANARY MUSEUM
KANARISCHES MUSEUM
KANARIEÖMUSEET

Dr. Vernan, 2. Es la más completa colección de vestigios de los habitantes prehispánicos de las Islas Canarias. Interesante sección de antropología, con momias, esqueletos, y cráneos aborígenes, destacando el tipo de Cro Magnon. Colección de cerámica, en la que destacan las «pintadoras», especie de sellos en terracota cuyos dibujos geométricos eran estampados en ocre y rojo sobre la piel y los vestidos de los antiguos canarios. Sección de flora y fauna.

Dr. Vernan, 2. C'est la collection la plus complète de vestiges des habitants préhispaniques des Iles Canaries. Une intéressante section d'antropologie, avec des momies, des squelettes et des crânes aborigènes, particulièrement le type de Cro Magnon. Collection de céramiques où sont remarquables les «pintadoras», sorte de sceaux en terre peinte, dont les dessins géométriques étaient imprimés en ocre et en rouge sur la peau et les vêtements des anciens canariens. Section de flore et de faune.

Dr. Vernan, 2. This has the fullest collection of the pre-hispanic inhabitants of the Canary Islands. An interesting section of anthropology, with mummies, skeletons and aborigine skulls, with the Cro Magnon type. A ceramics collection, with the famous «pintadoras» a kind of stamp in terracotta with geometric drawings printed in ochre and red on the skin, and the clothes of the ancient Canaries. Flora and Fauna section.

Dr. Vernan, 2. Es beherbergt die vollständigste Sammlung von Uberrresten der prehispanischen inselbewohner. Interessant ist die anthropologische Anteilung mit ihren Mumien, Skeletten und Schädel der Urbewohner, wobei besonders der Typ Cro Magnon hervorzuheben ist. In der Keramikabteilung sind vor allem sehenswert die sog. «pintadoras», Art Terracotta-Stempel, deren geometfrische ocker oder rotfarbigen Zeichnungen auf die Leder- oder Stoffbekleidung der Urbewohner aufgedruckt wurden Botanische und zoologische Anteilung.

Innehåller den mest fullständiga samlingen fornlämningar från tiden före öarna erövrades av Spanien. Antropologiavdelningen är intressant, med mumier, skelett och kranier av urinvånare, särskilt av Cro-Magnonrasen. Lergossamling, vari bör observeras ett slags sigill av terracotta, «pintadoras», vars geometriska mönster trycktes i ockra och rött på urinvånarnas hud och kläder. Avdelningar för flora och fauna.

CASA DE COLÓN
MAISON DE COLOMB
HOUSE OF COLUMBUS
HAUS DES KOLUMBUS
KOLUMBUSHUSET

Calle de Colón, 1. Antigua residencia de los primeros Gobernadores de la Isla. Posee el doble interés de su belleza arquitectónica y de la colección de objetos y documentos de la época colombina.

Rue de Colón, 1. Ancienne résidence des premiers Gouverneurs de l'île. Possède le double intérêt de sa beauté architecturale et de la collection d'objets et documents de l'époque de Colomb.

Calle de Colón, 1. The old residence of the first Governors of the Island. It is interesting for its architectural beauty as welt as for the collection of objects and documents from the Columbian period.

Calle de Colón, 1. Alte Residenz der ersten Gouverneure der Insel. Es ist duppelt interessant wegen seiner architektonischen Schönheil und wegen seiner Sammlung von Gegensfänden und Dokumenten aus der kolumbinischen Zeit.

Calle de Colón, 1. Antik residens av de första regerarna av ön. Residensens arkitektiska skönhet har det största värdet även samlingarna av föremal och dokumenter från den kolumbiska tiden.

CASA-MUSEO PÉREZ GALDÓS
MAISON-MUSÉE PÉREZ GALDÓS
PÉREZ GALDÓS HOUSE-MUSEUM
HAUS-MUSEUM PÉREZ GALDÓS
FODELSEHEMMET-MUSEUM PÉREZ GALDÓS

Calle Cano, 33. Se trata de la casa donde nació y vivió el gran novelista español, don Benito Pérez Galdós. Custodia manuscritos, epistolarios, dibujos, etc., y también otros recuerdos personales del ilustre escritor español.

Rue Cano, 33. Il s'agit de la maison où naquit et vécut le grand romancier espagnol, don Benito Pérez Galdós. Elle garde des manuscrits, des épistolaires, des dessins, etc., et aussi d'autres souvenirs personnels de l'illustre écrivain espagnol.

Calle Cano, 33. This is the house where the great Spanish novelist, don Benito Pérez Galdós, was born. It contains manuscripts, letters, drawings, etc., and other personal reminders of the famous Spanish writer.

Rue Cano, 33. Der grosse spanische Romanschriftsteller Benito Pérez Galdós wurde in diesem. Haus geboren und lebte dort. Es zeigt Manuskripte, gesammelte Briefe, Zeichnungen usw. und auch persönliche Dinge aus dem Besitz des berühmten spanischen Schritistellers.

Calle Cano, 33. I detta hus föddes och bodde den stora spanska författaren Benito Pérez Galdós. Här förvaras hans manuskript, brev och teckningar och även andra persontiga minnen.

MUSEO NÉSTOR
MUSÉE NÉSTOR
NÉSTOR MUSEUM
NÉSTOR-MUSEUM
NÉSTOR MUSEET

Se halla situado en el Pueblo Canario (Ciudad jardín). En él se exhiben óleos, dibujos, proyectos y, además, numerosos recuerdos personales, del pintor canario Néstor Martín-Fernández de la Torre (1888-1938).

Il se trouve situé dans le Pueblo Canario (Ciudad jardín). On y exhibe des peintures à l'huile, des dessins, des projets et, en outre, de nombreux souvenirs personnels du peintre canarien Néstor Martín-Fernández de la Torre (1888-1938).

It is located in the Canary Island Town (Ciudad jardín). Here are exhibited oil paintings, drawings, plans and many personal reminders of the Canary Island painter Néstor Martín-Fernández de la Torre (1888-1938).

Es befindet sich in dem Kanarischen Dorf (Ciudad jardín-Garfenstadt). Es werden dort Ölgemälde, Zeichnungen, Projekte und ausserdem viele persönliche Gegenstände des kanarischen Malers Néstor Martín-Fernández de la Torre (1888 bis 1938), gezeigt.

Detta museum ligger i själva staden (Ciudad jardín). I detta museum utställs oljemälningar, teckningar, planer samt ofaliga personliga minnen av den kanariska konstnären Néstor Martín-Fernández de la Torre (1888-1938).

MUSEO DIOCESANO DE ARTE SACRO
MUSÉE DIOCÉSAIN D'ART RELIGIEUX
DIOCESAN MUSEUM OF SACRED ART
DIÖZESANMUSEM DER HEILIGEN KUNST
STIFTSMUSEET FÖR RELIGIÖS KONST

Consta de seis salas, en las que se exponen magníficas pinturas flamencas y castellanas; esculturas y otros objetos de arte religioso, algunos de los cuales datan del siglo XV. Orfebrería hispano-americana, tapices aztecas y muebles de época. Muchas de estas obras son de gran valor, destacando un Crucifijo atribuido a Alonso Cano, una valiosa colección de imágenes de tallistas canarios de los siglos XVII y XVIII, y un Calvario del escultor canario Luján Pérez.

Formé par six salles où l'on expose de magnifiques peintures flamandes et castillanes; sculptures et d'autres objets d'art religieux, dont certains datent du XVème siècle. Orfèvrerie hispano-américaine, tapis aztèques et mobilier de l'époque. Beaucoup de ces oeuvres sont de grande valeur, et parmi les plus remarquables on y trouve un Crucifix attribué à Alonso Cano, une estimable collection de sculptures des ciseleurs canariens des XVIIème et XVIIIème siècles et un Calvaire du sculpteur canarien Luján Pérez.

Formed by six halls where magnificent Flemish and Castillian paintings can be admired; sculptures and other works of religious art, some of them dating from the XV Century, Spanish-American gold smith works, Aztec tapestry and furniture from that time. Many of these works are of great value, among the most remarkable a Crucifix attributed to Alonso Cano, a valuable collection of images made by Canarian woodcarvers of the XVII and XVIII Centuries, and a Calvary made by the Canarian sculptor Luján Pérez.

Bestehend aus sechs Sälen in den ausgezeichnete flämische und kastilische Gemälde ausgestellt sind; Skulpturen und endere Werke der heiligen Kunst, manchè von ihnen aus den XV Jahrhundert stammend, Spanischamerikanische Goldschmiedearbeil, aztekische Teppische und Möbel aus jener Zeit. Viele von diesen Werken sind von grossem Wert, besonders ein Kruzifix welches Alonso Cano zugeschrieben wird, eine kostbare Sammlung von Heiligenbildern kanarischer Künstler aus den XVII und XVIII Jahrhunderten und ein Leidensweg des Kanarischen Bildhauers Luján Pérez.

Sex salar med magnifika flamländska och kastilianska tavlor, skulpturer och andra religiösa konstföremål, av vilka några är från 1400-talet. Latinamerikansk guldsmideskonst, aztekiska väggbonader, och stilmöbler. Många av dessa föremål är mycket värdefulla, särskilt bör märkas ett krucifix som förmodas vara gjort av Alonso Cano, en förnämlig samlig helgonfigurer av loka la träsnidare från 1600- och 1700-talet, samt ett verk av skulptören Luján Pérez, föreställande Kristi korsfästelse.

1.3. BIBLIOTECAS
   BIBLIOTHEQUES
   LIBRARIES
   BIBLIOTHEKEN
   BIBLIOTEK

Las Palmas

BIBLIOTECA PÚBLICA INSULAR, Tomás Morales, 96.
BIBLIOTECA MUNICIPAL «ESCALERITA». Dr. Fleming (Escaleritas).
BIBLIOTECA MUNICIPAL «PUERTO DE LA LUZ». Américo Vespucio, 43.
BIBLIOTECA MUNICIPAL «SANTA CATALINA». Guayedra, 15.
BIBLIOTECA DEL MUSEO CANARIO. Dr. Chil 33.
BIBLIOTECA DEL SEMINARIO CONCILIAR. Dr. Chil, 25.
BIBLIOTECA PÉREZ GALDÓS. Cano, 33.
BIBLIOTECA BALLESTEROS. Casa de Colón.

Lanzarote

BIBLIOTECA MUNICIPAL. Arrecife.

1.4. ARTESANÍA
ARTISANAT
GRAFTWORK
KUNSTHANDWERK
KONSTHANTVERK

El gusto del pueblo también se manifiesta en su artesanía. Sus bordados y cerámicas son resultado de una vieja tradición que se conserva en muchos pueblos del interior. Se fabrican también cestos de hoja de palma, tejidos de lana y de lino, objetos fallados en madera y cuchillos canarios de empuñadura finamente labrada. Actualmente la manufactura de cigarros, que ha conseguido una alta reputación internacional, es la más reciente expresión de la maestría artesana del isleño.

Le goût populaire se manifeste aussi dans l'artisanat. Les broderies et les céramiques sont le fruit d'une vielle tradition conservée dans beaucoup de villages de l'intérieur. On fabrique aussi des paniers avec des feuilles de palmier, des tissus de laine et de lin, des objets taillés dans le bois et des couteaux canariens au manche finement ouvré. La fabrication des cigares et cigarettes, qui est la plus récente manifestacion de la maîtrise artisanale insulaire, a attcint une haute réputation internationale.

Their embroidery qnd ceramics have inherited an age-old tradition that has survived in many inland villages. Other products of their craftsmanship include palm-leaf baskets, wool and linen materials, wood-carvings and Canary-Island knives with intricately designed hilts. The latest illustration of the islanders' skills is the production of cigars that have wan high reputations throughout the world.

Der Geschmack des Volkes kommf auch in seinem Handwerk zum Ausdruck. Seine Stickereien und Keramikarbeiten sind das Ergebnis einer alten Tradition, die sich in vielen Dörfern des Inneren erhalten hat. Es werden auch aus Palmblättern Körbe hergestellt, Stoffe aus Wolle und Leinen, holzgeschnitzte Gegenstände und kanarische Messer mit fein ausgeführtem Griff. Gegenwärtig ist die Zigarettenfabrikation, die einen hohen internationalen Ruf eelangt hat, der jüngste Ausdruck der handwerklichen Fertigkeit der Inselbewohner.

Folkets goda smak tar sig också uttryck i konsthantverket. Broderier och keramikarbeten har en gammal tradition som fortfarande bevaras i många byar inåt *land*. Man tillverkar *också* korgar av palmblad, lin- och ylletyger, snidade träföremål och typiska knivar med fint arbetat fäste. För närvarande är cigarrtill-

verkningen, som vunnit stor internationell ryktbarhet, den senast tillkomna yttringen av öbornas mästerskap på konsthantverkets område.

2. ALOJAMIENTOS
LOGEMENTS
ACCOMODATION
UNTERKUNFTE
HOTELL OCH PENSIONAT

2.1. HOTELES
HÔTELS
HOTELS
HOTELS
HOTELLER

Categoría 5 Estrellas. Categorie 5 Étolles. 5 Star Category. Kategorie 5 Sterne. 1.ª Klass Hotell.

Las Palmas

CRISTINA. Gomera, 4.
REINA ISABEL. P. de las Canteras.
SANTA CATALINA. Parque Doramas.

**Maspalomas
(San Bartolomé de Tirajana)**

MASPALOMAS OASIS. Playa de Maspalomas.
TAMARINDOS. Playa de San Agustín.

Lanzarote

SALINAS, LAS. Maleza de Tahiche. **Teguise.**

Fuerteventura

YBARRA TRES ISLAS. Playa de Corralejo. **Corralejo.**

Categoría 4 Estrellas. Categorie 4 Étolles. 4 Star Category. Kategorie 4 Sterne. 2.ª Klass Hotell.

Las Palmas

CONCORDE. Tomás Miller 8 y 10.
DON JUAN. Eduardo Benot, 3.
IBERIA. Avda. Marítima del Norte.
IMPERIAL PLAYA. Ferreras, 1.
MIRAFLOR. Dr. Grau Bassas, 21.
LAS PALMAS PALACE. León y Castillo, 414.
ROCAMAR. Lanzarote, 8.
SANSOFE. Portugal, 68.
SOL. 29 de Abril, 87.
TIGADAY. Ripoche, 4.

Maspalomas
San Bartolomé de Tirajana

APOLO. Avda. EE. UU., 20.
CASERÍO, EL. Avda. de Italia, 8.
CATARINA PLAYA. Avda. de Tirajana, s/n.
COSTA CANARIA. Ctra. del Sur, km 61.
DON GRECORY. Las Tabaibas.
EUGENIA VICTORIA. Playa del Inglés.
FARO DE MASPALOMAS. Playa de Maspalomas.
FOLIAS. Playa de San Agustín.
IFA DUNAMAR. Playa del Inglés.
LUCANA. Plaza del Sol.
MARGARITAS, LAS. Avda. Gran Canaria, s/n.
PALM BEACH. Playa de Maspalomas.

Lanzarote

ARRECIFE GRAN HOTEL. Avda. Mancomunidad, s/n. **Arrecife.**
LOS FARIONES. Puerto del Carmen, s/n. **Arrecife.**
SAN ANTONIO. Playa los Pocillos. Tías.

Fuerteventura

ROBINSÓN CLUB JANDIA PLAYA. Playa de Janchá. **Pajara.**

Categoría 3 Estrellas. Categorie 3 Étoiles.
3 Star Category. Kategorie 3 Sterne.
3ᵈⁱᵉ Klass Hotell

Las Palmas

ABANIKO. J. Mesa y López.
ASTORIA. Pelayo, 23.
ATLANTA. Alfredo L. Jones, 43.
ATLÁNTICO. Dr. García Castrillo, 20.
BALLESMEN. León y Castillo, 423.
BAÑOSOL. Portugal, 91.
BEGOÑA. Portugal, 68.
BRASILIA. Faro, 12 y 14.
BYBLOS. Albareda, 108.
LA CALETA. Fco. González Díaz, 5.
CANTUR. Sagasta, 30.
LAS CARACOLAS. La Palma, 2.
CÉSAR. León Tolstoi, 2.
CORINTO. Prudencio Morales, 47.
FARO. Faro, 16.
FRANDORI. Gral. Primo de Rivera, 39.
GARMÓN. Galicia, 15.
GRAN CANARIA. Avda. Las Canteras, 38.
HELIOS. Isla de Cuba, 6.
IDAFE. Nicolás Estébanez, 49.
JOCAHE. León Tolstoi.
LAS LANZAS. Bernardo de la Torre, 17.
LUMI. Colombia, 14.
MALOMY. Nicolás Estébanez, 63.
MARASU. Dr. García Castrillo, 13.
NICO-PLAYA. Sagasta, 108.
OLIMPIA. Dr. Grau Bassas, 1.

PINITO DEL ORO. Portugal, 30.
RIVIERA. Joaquín Costa, 67.
ROSALÍA. Dr. Miguel Rosas, 3.
SEMIRAMIS. Dr. Grau Bassas, 39.
SORIMBA. Portugal, 26.
TENESOYA. Sagasta, 98.
TROCADERO. Los Martínez de Escobar, 81.
UTIACA. Albareda, 35.
LAS VELAS. Prudencio Morales, 61.
VILLA BLANCA. Alfredo L. Jones, 39.

Caldera de Bandama
(Santa Brígida)

LA POSADA. Caldera de Bandama, s/n.

Maspalomas-Costa Canaria
(San Bartolomé de Tirajana)

BEVERLY PARK. Playa del Inglés.
BUENAVENTURA PLAYA. Plaza Ansite, s/n.
PARQUE TROPICAL. Avda. Italia, s/n.
PROTUCASA PLAYA DEL INGLÉS. Playa del Inglés.
REY CARLOS. Playa del Inglés.
WAIKIKI. Playa del Inglés.
YBARRA DON MIGUEL. Avda. Tirajana, s/n.

Lanzarote

Arrecife

LANCELOT PLAYA. Avda. Mancomunidad, s/n.
MIRAMAR. Coll, 2.
CARDONA. Igualadad, s/n.

Fuerteventura

Puerto del Rosario

LAS GABIAS. Avda. Marítima, 3.

Punta Jandía-Tuineje

CASA ATLÁNTICA. Playa del Matorral.

Tarajalejo

MAXORATA. Ctra. Tarajalejo.

Categoría 2 Estrellas. Categorie 2 Étoiles.
2 Star Category. Kategorie 2 Sterne.
4ᵈⁱᵉ Klass Hotell

Las Palmas

LAS ALGAS. Gravina, 20.
ALVA. Alfredo Jones, 33.
AROMAS. Faro, 1.
BRAEMAR. Luis Morote, 29.
CACTUS. Juan Rejón, 23.
EL CISNE. Ferreras, 19.
DAMASCO. 29 de Abril, 6.
FUNCHAL. Los Martínez Escobar, 68.
LOS GERANIO. Paseo Tomás Morales, 165.
GERMÁN. Faro, 66.

HESPERIDES. La Naval, 7.
LUIS MOROTE. Luis Morote, 13.
MAJORICA. Ripoche, 22.
MAROLA. Ferreras, 23.
NAUTILUS. Paseo de las Canteras, 5.
NUBIA. Pedro del Castillo, 10.
PRINCESA. Princesa Guayarmina, 2 y 4.
PUJOL. Salvador Cuyas, 5.
RETAMA. Padre Cueto, 15.
ROMPEOLAS. Portugal, 60.
SYRIA. Luis Morote, 27.
TAGOR. Sagasta, 60.
TANAGUA. Sagasta, 92.
VALENCIA. Valencia, 64.

Cruz de Tejeda

PARADOR NACIONAL CRUZ DE TEJEDA. A 9 km de Tejeda.

Maspalomas-Costa Canaria (San Bartolomé de Tirajana)

ESCORIAL. El Veril Playa del Inglés.
INTER CLUB ATLANTIC. Jazmines, 4.
PARAÍSO MASPALOMAS. Playa del Inglés.
SAHARA PALAYA. Playa del Inglés.

Mogán

PUERTO PLATA. Urb. Puerto Rico.

Santa Brígida

SANTA BRIGIDA. Ctra. del Centro.

Tarifa Baja

MIRALUZ. Ctra. del Centro, 10.

Lanzarote

Arrecife

AVENIDA. Avda. Mancomunidad, 30.
TAMIA. Avenida.

Yaiza

PLAYA BLANCA. Playa Blanca, s/n.
PLAYA DEL SOL. Playa Blanca.

Fuerteventura

Puerto del Rosario

PARADOR NACIONAL DE FUERTEVENTURA. Playa Blanca.
ROQUE MAR. León y Castillo, s/n.
TAMASITE. León y Castillo, 9.

Pajara

OBEROL CASA ATLÁNTICA. Jandía Playa.

2.2. APARTAMENTOS TURÍSTICOS
APPARTEMENTS TOURISTIQUES
TOURIST APARTMENTS
APARTEMENTHAUSER
SEMESTERVANINGAR

Las Palmas

DORESTE. Maestro Valle, 15.
SANTA MÓNICA. Paseo del Chil, 79.
FLORIDA. Paseo de Chil, 77.
CASA SUECIA. Luis Morote.
LOS DRAGOS. Alonso Quesada, 10.
TORRE DEL VIENTO. Playa de La Laja, 23.
MACÍAS. Pin y Margall, 25.
OFELIA. Blasco Ibáñez, 19.
CASA APARTAMENTOS. Juan Rejón, 43.
BONNY. Juan Rejón, 97.
FARILAGA. Paseo de Las Canteras, 54.
REINA. Fuerteventura, 12.
VIKINGOS. Pedro del Castillo, 24.
VILLA EDÉN. Mirador de Escaleritas.
LAS PALMERAS. Plaza Emilio Ley.
EMILIO. La Naval, 4.
ROBLEDANO. Grau Bassas, 38.
MARAVILLA. Secretario Artiles, 27.
COSTA DEL SOL. Prudencio Morales, 17.
SANTA CATALINA. León y Castillo, 337.

Lanzarote

Arrecife

ARRECIFE PLAYA. Avda. de la Mancomunidad, 10. 1.ª C.
ISLAMAR. Avda. de la Mancomunidad. 2.ª C.
MARIS. José Bertancort, 7. 2.ª C.
RUBICON. Avda. de la Mancomunidad, 16. 2.ª C.
ISABEL. Francos, 4 y 6. 3.ª C.
PARQUE. Gral. Franco, s/n. 3.ª C.
PLAYA. Avda. de la Mancomunidad, s/n. Bloque B. 3.ª C.

Tías

CIUDAD JARDÍN MIRAMAR. Apartado 219-Arrecife. 2.ª C.

Fuerteventura

Punta Jandía (Tuineje)

CLUB MARABU. Valle de Esquinzo, 1.ª C.

2.3. CAMPINGS

LA PARDILLA. Ctra. Las Palmas-Gando, km 11.
GUANTÁNAMO. Playa de Tauro.
TEMISAS. Lomo La Cruz.

3. GASTRONOMÍA
   GASTROMIE
   GASTRONOMY
   GASTRONOMIE
   GASTRONOMI

3.1. RESTAURANTES
   RESTAURANTS
   RESTAURANTS
   RESTAURANTS
   RESTAURANGER

Gran Canaria

Cocina española
Cuisine espagnole
Spanish cooking
Spanische Küche
Spanskt Kök

BODEGÓN DEL PUEBLO CANARIO. Pueblo
   Canario. 2.ª C.
EL LASSO (especialidades canarias). Lomo del
   Lasso, 2.ª C.
LA PEÑA. Parque de Santa Catalina. 3.ª C.
EL GUANCHE. Parque de Santa Catalina. 2.ª C.
EL RAYO. Ripoche, 3. 2.ª C.
EL TIMPLE. Dr. Miguel Rosa, 10. 3.ª C.
IKEA. (Especialidades vascas.) Joaquín Costa,
   26. 2.ª C.
JUAN PÉREZ. Prudencio Morales, 17. 2.ª C.
JARDÍN CANARIO. Carretera del Centro, km 7.
   2.ª C.
LAS CUEVAS DE ARTILES. Las Meleguinas
   (Santa Brígida).
LA TROPICAL. Barranco Seco, carretera del
   Centro, km 3. 2.ª C.
MESÓN LA PAELLA. José M.ª Durán, 47. 3.ª C.
ARROYO. Prudencio Morales, 37. 2.ª C.

Cocina italiana
Cuisine italienne
Italian cooking
Italienische Küche
Italienskt Kök.

LA PIZZA. Tomás Miller, 64. 3.ª C.
LA PIZZA REAL. Mas de Gaminde, 11. 2.ª C.
MILANES. Albareda, 26. 3.ª C.

Cocina escandinava
Cuisine scandinave
Scandinavian cooking
Skandinavische Küche
Skandinaviskt Kök

TRES CORONAS. Sagasta, 80. 1.ª C.
TERRAZA (autoservicio). Luis Morote, 46. 2.ª C.
DON QUIJOTE. Secretario Artiles, 74. 2.ª C.
COLÓN PLAYA. Alfredo L. Jones, 53. 2.ª C.

BALDAQUÍN (autoservicio). Sargento Llagas,
   28. 2.ª C.
CASAKANT. Portugal, 13. 1.ª C.

Cocina francesa
Cuisine française
French cooking
Französische Küche
Franskt Kök

EL RANCHO. Nicolás Estévanez, 40. 3.ª C.
FATAGA. Galicia, 21. 2.ª C.
LA CREPRY. Luis Morote, 35. 2.ª C.

Cocina oriental
Cuisine orientale
Oriental cooking
Orientalische Küche
Orientaliskt Kök

HOUSE-MING. Paseo de las Canteras, 30. 2.ª C.
CHINA. Sagasta, 12. 2.ª C.
FORMOSA. Torres Quevedo, 26. 2.ª C.
FUJI. Fernando Guanarteme, 56. 2.ª C.
PANTAI. Sargento Llagas, 20 3.ª C.
GOLDEN GATE (Puerta Dorada). Tenerife, 22.
   3.ª C.
EL SUBMARINO. Paseo de las Canteras, 5.
   2.ª C.
MANKING. General Primo de Rivera, 11. 2.ª C.
SALÓN DE CHINA. Ripoche, 9. 2.ª C.

Cocina internacional
Cuisine internationale
International cooking
Internationale Küche
Internationelt Kök

VILLA EDÉN. Paseo de la Cornisa, 4. 1.ª C.
SUIZO. Sargento Llagas, 37. 1.ª C.
COSTA BELLA. Paseo de las Canteras, 3. 2.ª C.
PINITO DEL ORO. Portugal, 30. 2.ª C.
COLUMBUS. Bernardo de la Torre, 71. 2.ª C.
PAMPA GRILL (asados). Colombia, 6. 2.ª C.
FERIA DEL ATLÁNTICO. Lomo del Polvo. 2.ª C.
LES AMBASSADEURS. Nicolás Estévanez, 52.
   2.ª C.
BEGOÑA. Portugal, 62. 2.ª C.
LA GUITARRA. Dr. Miguel Rosa, 21. 1.ª C.
PIO PIO (asados). Sargento Llagas, 1. 2.ª C.
MARFIL PLAYA. Paseo de las Canteras, 9. 2.ª C.
HOGAR DEL ASADO (asados). Los Martínez
   Escobar, 37. 3.ª C.
ACUARIO. Pi y Margall, 23. 2.ª C.
DON PEDRO. Tenerife, 22. 2.ª C.
HAMBURG. General Orgaz, 54. 2.ª C.
TÍO LUIS (UNCLE LOUIS). Sargento Llagas, 18.
   3.ª C.
LOS CEDROS (especialidades árabes). Los
   Martínez de Escobar, 68. 2.ª C.
PANAMÉRICAN II. La Estrella, carretera del
   Sur, km 12. 3.ª C.

Agaete

ANTONIO. Puerto de las Nieves. 3.ª C.
CAPITA. Puerto de las Nieves. 3.ª C.

Artenara

MESÓN LA SILLA. La Montañeta, s/n. 2.ª C.

Arucas

MESÓN DE LA MONTAÑA. La Montaña. 2.ª C.
ESTACIÓN. Suárez Franchy, s/n. 3.ª C.
QUINTANILLA. Calle 810 (Quintanilla). 3.ª C.
GUERRA. Suárez Franchy, s/n. 4.ª C.

Carrizal

SANTANA. Zorrilla, 3. 4.ª C.

Gáldar

LA FRAGATA. Playa de la Sardina. 3.ª C.
PARADA. Ctra. Las Palmas-Agaete, km 40.
    3.ª C.
VISTA MAR. Playa de Sardina del Norte, s/n.
    3.ª C.
EL AGUJERO. Playa del Agujero. 4.ª C.
HERMANOS VEGA. Capitán Quesada, 24. 4.ªC.

Galdina

GUILLERMO. Playa de Sardina. 4.ª C.

Gando

LA LUNA. C-812, km 24,800. 1.ª C.

Guanarteme

LAS ROCAS. Secretario Padilla, 33. 3.ª C.

Maspalomas

ASADERO DE POLLOS CONTE. Playa de Mas-
    palomas. 4.ª C.
LITORAL. Avda. de las Américas, s/n. 4.ª C.
CASA COMIDA. Ctra. General Maspalomas.
    4.ª C.

Mogán

PUERTO RICO. Playa de Puerto Rico. 2.ª C.
CASTILLA. Arguineguin. P. K 67, C-812. 3.ª C.

San Bartolomé de Tirajana

LA ROTONDA. Playa de San Agustín, s/n. L.
MONTE DEL MORO. Playa de San Agustín, s/n.
    1.ª C.
LAS OLAS. Playa del Inglés. 1.ª C.
LAS ARENAS. Playa del Inglés. 2.ª C.
LORO VERDE. Playa Honda. 2.ª C.
MASPALOMAS. Playa de Maspalomas. 2.ª C.
EL PETIT. El Veril. 2.ª C.

San Mateo

EL REFUGIO. Cruz de Tejeda, s/n. 2.ª C.
GUINIGUADA. Ctra. 814, km 35,200. 3.ª C.

PEÑAGÓN. El Retiro. 3.ª C.
LOS PINOS. El Retiro, s/n. 3.ª C.
EL SAUCILLO. Retiro, 4. 3.ª C.
LOS FAROLITOS. Lomo de la Rosa, km 27,850.
    4.ª C.
EL RETIRO MERENDERO. El Retiro, 1. 4.ª C.

Santa Brígida

BENTAYGA. Monte, 66. 2.ª C.
VIKING. Ctra. C-811, km 11. 2.ª C.
GUAYEDRA. Ctra. del Centro, 75. 3.ª C.
MANO DE HIERRO. Vuelta del Pino, 8. 3.ª C.
EL PALMERAL. Ctra. Santa Brígida-Calzada.
    3.ª C.
FALCÓN. Portada Verde, km 15,750. 4.ª C.

Santa Lucía

HAO. Ctra. 815, km 51,200. 3.ª C.
ESTRELLA DE ORO. Cruce de Sardina del Sur.
    3.ª C.
EL PEÑÓN. San Rafael del Vecindario. 4.ª C.
SURESTE. General Franco, s/n. 4.ª C.

Tafira

RIO MIÑO. Murillo, 1. 2.ª C.

Telde

AEROPUERTO. Ctra. C-812, km 26. 1.ª C.
LA CABAÑA. Ctra. C-812, km 24,100. 3.ª C.
ROCA EDÉN. Rosa, 39. 3.ª C.
CASA DAVID. Valle de los Nueve, s/n. 4.ª C.
MARRAKECH. Palya de la Garita, s/n. 4.ª C.

Teror

LA ROSALEDA. General Franco, 16. 3.ª C.

Valleseco

LOS ROQUETES. Ctra. C-814, km 26. 2.ª C.
VALLESECO. Zamora. 3.ª C.

Valsequillo

LA CARAVANA. La Barrera, km 55. 4.ª C.
EL SAUZAL. José Antonio, s/n. 4.ª C.

Marisquerías. Fruits de mer.
Sea food. Seemuscheln.
Restaurant specialiserad i havsmusslor

EL TROVADOR. Sagasta, 66.
JULIO. La Naval, 132.
SAN RAFAEL. Paseo de Escaleritas, 102.
NUEZ. Kasbah (Playa del Inglés). Carretera del
    Sur, km 54.

Lanzarote

Arrecife

COSTA BRAVA. Avda. General Franco, 4. 3.ª C.
GUANAPAY. Fajardo, 38. 3.ª C.

LOS LAJARES. León y Castillo, 40. 3.ª C.
RINCÓN DEL MAJO. Aquilino Fernández, 20.
   3.ª C.
TISALAYA. Pérez Galdós, 12. 3.ª C.
LOS CANARIOS. León y Castillo, 39. 4.ª C.
EL MESÓN DE LOS POLLOS. Canalejas, 56.
   4.ª C.
EL MOLINO. Puerto Naos. 4.ª C.
LA PEÑA. León y Castillo, 48. 4.ª C.
SAINT TROPEZ. General Franco, 16. 4.ª C.

Tías

BARRACUDA. Urb. Playa Blanca, S. A. 1.ª C.

Teguise

FAMARA. Playa de Famara, s/n. 2.ª C.
ACATIFE. San Miguel, 4. 3.ª C.
LA GALERA. Las Caletas, km 4. 3.ª C.

Tinajo

MONTAÑA DEL FUEGO. Montaña del Fuego.
   2.ª C.
LA SANTA. Urb. La Santa. 2.ª C.

Yaiza

CASA SALVADOR. Playa Balnca. 3.ª C.
LA ERA. Yaiza. 3.ª C.
EL VOLCÁN. Plaza de los Remedios, 4. 3.ª C.
TIMANFAYA. Barrio de Uga. 4.ª C.

Fuerteventura

Corralejo

LA GALERA. Corralejo. 2.ª C.

3.2. ESPECIALIDADES GASTRONÓMICAS
SPÉCIALITÉS GASTRONOMIQUES
GASTRONOMIC SPECIALITIES
SPEZIALITATEN GASTRONOMISCHE
GASTRONOMISKA SPECIALITETER

El gofio (harina de maíz tostado) constituye el
alimento básico de los campesinos. Su em-
pleo es muy variado, utilizándose en la pre-
paración de dos platos típicos: «salcocho» y
«caldo de pescado».
El mojo es una salsa picante a base de
aceite, vinagre, sal y especias, que figura
como condimento indispensable en numerosos platos canarios.
Otras especialidades de la cocina canaria
son: el puchero, el pescado embarrado, el
cabrito en adobo; y entre los postres hay que
mencionar el queso de Guía, las rapaduras,
el frangollo y la sopa de Ingenio.
Entre los vinos, de alta graduación y sabor
característico, debido al terreno volcánico,
merecen destacarse los del Monte y la mal-
vasía de Lanzarote, y entre los licores, el ron
y las típicas «guindillas».

Le gofio est l'aliment de base des campagnards
(farine de mais rotie). Son emploi est très va-
rié, et il est utilisé dans la préparation de
deux palts typiques: «salcocho» et «caldo de
pescado».
Le mojo est une sauce piquante à base
d'huile, vinaigre, sel et épices, qui figure
comme condiment indispensable dans de
nombreux plats canariens. D'autres spéciali-
tés de la cuisine canarienne sont: le puchero
(pot au feu), le poisson «embarrado», le che-
vreau en daube; et parmi les déserts il faut
mentionner le fromage de Guía, les «rapaduras», le «frangollo» et la «sopa de Ingenio».
Parmi les vins, de haute graduation et saveur
caractéristiques en raison du terrain volcanique, il faut distinguer ceux du Monte et la
malvoisie de Lanzarote, et parmi les liqueurs,
le rhum et les typiques «guindillas».

«Gofio» (toasted corn fluor) is the basic food of
the country people. It has a great variety of
uses, but is specially found in the preparation
of two typical dishes: «salcocho» and «caldo
de pescado».
«Mojo» is a hot, spicy sauce made from oil,
vinegar, salt and herbs, that is used as a necessary addition to many Canary Island dishes. Other specialities include: «puchero»,
«embarrado» fish, «cabrito en adobo»; from
among the many different desserts, we must
mention the cheese of Guia, the «rapaduras»,
the «frangollo» and the «sopa de Ingenio».
The wines are high grade with a characteristic flavor, due to the volcanic land. Outstanding are those from the Monte, and the
malmsey wine from Lanzarote, there are also
the typical «guindillas» and rum.

Der «gofio» (gerostetes Maismehl) ist das
Hauptnahrungsmittel der Landbevolkerung.
Es wird auf viele verschiedene Arten verwandt
und dient zur Zuvereifung von zwei typischen
Gerichten: «salcocho» und «caldo de pesca-
do» (Fischsuppe).
«El mojo» ist eine pikante Sosseie mit Ol,
Essig, Salz und Gewurzen zubereitet und ist:
sie ist bei zahlreichen kananischen Gerichten
als Wirze unentbehrlich.
Andere Spezialitäten der kanarischen Küche
sind: «el puchero», «el pescado embarrado»
(Fischgericht), «el cabrito en adobo» (Zie-
genbraten in Würze); unter den Nachtischen
ist besonders zu erwähnen: Der Käse von
Guía, «las rapaduras», «el frangollo» (Mais-
gericht) und «la sopa de Ingenio».
Unter den Weiner, die hochgradig sind und
dank des vulkanischen Bodens einen charak-
terischen Geschmack haben, verdienen besonders erwahnt zu werden: die Weine vom
Monte und die Malvasierweine von Lanzarote: unter den Likören der Rum und die typischen «guindillas».

El Gofio (brynt maismjöl) är lantbefolkningens grundnäring. Det finns många olika variationer att tillreda en rätt av mjölet. De två mest typiska rätterna är: «salcocho» (ingredienser: cherre, en slags fisk som bör vara torkad och osaltad, kokta potatis med skal, gofio preparerad med est samt med en fiskbuljong. Man brukar även tillsätta lite av «mojo»). Därefter «Caldo de pescado», fiskbuljong. El mojo är en sås som kan vara lite eller mycket kryddad. Ingredienser: olja, salt, vinäger, malen paprika samt kryddor från ön, variation: Mojo verde (grön mojo) med olja, lite vinäger, persil, vitlök och de typiska kryddorna från ön. Denna sås är oundvikling bland befolkningens matvanor. Andra specialiteter från öarna: «el puchero» (grönsaker, potatis, kött, korv. Allt detta kokas tillsammans i ett lerkärl).

«El pescado embarrado», friterad fisk med en sås gjord av tomater, stekt lök, paprika, därtill äter man kokta potatissar. «El cabrito en adobo» (en liten get, mindre än sju kilo, som man anräthar med vitlök, vin, lagerblad och andra aromatiska kryddor). Bland efterrätterna bör man nämna osten fran Guía (gjord av mjölken fran kon, geten och fåret, allt sammanort). «Las rapaduras» en konfekt gjord av gofio, honung och med mandel. «El frangollo», en efterrätt gjord av kokt maismjöl, när det väl är kallt tillsätter man mjölk, honung eller socker. Vinena är mycket starka och med en särskild smak, detta tack var den vulganiska joarten. Av de många vinsorterna bör man nämna vinerna fran Monte och malvoisier-vinet, detta vin från Lanzarote. Alkoholerna, öarnas rom och de typiska «guindillas» (körsbärslikör).

AUSTRIA. Juan Rejón, 89, 1.°.
BÉLGICA. Leopoldo Matos, 22, ent. 1.° izq.
COLOMBIA. Triana, 120, 2.°.
COREA. León Tolstoi, 1, 4.°.
CUBA. León y Castillo, 247.
CHILE. Barcelona, 35, 1.°.
DINAMARCA. Concepción Arenal, 20 (Ed. Cantabria).
EL SALVADOR. Perdomo, 11.
ESTADOS UNIDOS. General Primo de Rivera, 5.
FILIPINAS. Doctor Chil, 20.
FINLANDIA. G. Más de Gaminde, 45, 1.°.
FRANCIA. Néstor de la Torre, 12.
GRAN BRETAÑA. Alfredo L. Jones, 33, 6.°.
GRECIA. Casa Miller. Muelle Sta. Catalina.
GUATEMALA. León y Castillo, 79.
HOLANDA. León y Castillo, 244, 6.°.
INDIA. Triana, 24.
ISLANDIA. Juan de Escobedo, 5.
ITALIA. Mariucha, 2 A.
JAPÓN. Santiago Rusiñol, 12.
LÍBANO. Eusebio Navarro, 25.
LIBERIA. Pérez Galdós, 43, 1.°.
MARRUECOS. Avda. Mesa y López, 8, 2.°.
MAURITANIA. Juan E. Doreste, 11 (Vegueta).
MÓNACO. León y Castillo, 253.
NICARAGUA. San Nicolás, 18, 1.° 1.ª.
NORUEGA. Maestro Valle, 22.
PERÚ. Mesa y López, 1.
PORTUGAL. Paseo Tomás Morales, 67, 5.°.
REPÚBLICA DOMINICANA. J. de León y Joven, 14.
SENEGAL. Lope de Vega, 2.
SIERRA LEONA. Viera y Clavijo, 34, 3.° I.
SIRIA. León y Castillo, 189, 3.°.
SUDÁFRICA. Albareda, 50.
SUECIA. Presidente Alvear, 52, 2.°.
SUIZA. El Cid, 38.
URUGUAY. Triana, 60, 4.°.

4. AGENDA PRÁCTICA
AGENDA PRATIQUE
PRACTICAL AGENDA
PRAKTISCHES NACHSCHLAGEWERK
PRAKTISKA TIPS

4.1. CONSULADOS
CONSULATS
CONSULATES
KONSULATE
KONSULAT

ALEMANIA. General Primo de Rivera, 5, 2.° puertas 3-4.
ARGENTINA. General Primo de Rivera, 5, 2.° oficina 10.

4.2. DIRECCIONES Y SERVICIOS ÚTILES
ADRESSES ET SERVICES UTILES
USEFUL ADDRESSES AND SERVICES
NÖTZLICHE ADRESSEN UND DIENSTE
NYTTIGA ADRESSER

**Correos. Postes. Post Offices
Postamer. Post**

LAS PALMAS. General Franco, 62.
LANZAROTE. Avda. Gral. Franco. Arrecife.
FUERTEVENTURA. León y Castillo, s/n. Puerto Rosario.

**Succursales. Succursales
Branch Offices. Zweigstellen
Filialer**

LAS PALMAS. Puerto de la Luz. Albareda, 79.

Telégrafos. Télégraphes
Telegraph Offices. Telegraphenämer
Telegraf

LAS PALMAS. General Franco, 62.
LANZAROTE. Avda. Gral. Franco. Arrecife.
FUERTEVENTURA. León y Castillo, s/n. Puerto
  Rosario.

Sucursales. Succursales
Branch Offices. Zweigstellen
Filialer

LAS PALMAS. Puerto de La Luz. Dr. Miguel
  Rosas, 22.

Teléfonos. Téléphones
Telephone Exchanges. Telephonamt
Och Telefon

LAS PALMAS. General Primo de Rivera, 11.
LANZAROTE. José Antonio, 5. Arrecife.
FUERTEVENTURA. García Hernández, 6.
  Puerto Rosario.

Sucursales. Succursales
Branch Offices. Zweigstellen
Filialer

LAS PALMAS. León y Castillo, 275. Domingo J.
  Navarro, 30.

Teléfonos de urgencia
Téléphones d'urgence
Emergency-telephone numbers
Notrufe
Nöd Telefoner

Las Palmas (Gran Canaria)

POLICÍA NACIONAL. Telf. 36 11 66.
CASA DE SOCORRO. Telf. 24 51 57.
BOMBEROS. Telf. 24 31 00.
AYUNTAMIENTO. Telf. 31 50 22.
GUARDIA CIVIL. Telf. 31 08 87.
POLICÍA MUNICIPAL. Telf. 20 22 27.

Arrecife (Lanzarote)

POLICÍA NACIONAL. Telf. 81 13 02.
CASA DE SOCORRO. Telf. 81 05 00.
BOMBEROS. Telf. 81 10 60.
GUARDIA CIVIL. Telf. 81 09 46.
POLICÍA MUNICIPAL. Telf. 81 13 17.

Puerto del Rosario (Fuerteventura)

POLICÍA NACIONAL. Telf. 85 09 09.
CASA DE SOCORRO. Telf. 85 07 70.
GUARDIA CIVIL. Telf. 85 05 03.
POLICÍA MUNICIPAL. Telf. 85 06 35.

Comunicaciones
Communications
Communications
Verkehrsverbindungen
Kommunikationer

Autobuses. Autobus
Buses. Autobusse
Bussar

Gran Canaria

Servicios de autobuses regulares de
  UTINSA y SALCAI. Salidas desde la calle
  Rafael Cabrera, frente al Parque San
  Telmo.

Carretera del Norte

Las Palmas-Arucas y regreso. Las Palmas-
  Teror y regreso. Las Palmas-Valleseco.
  Valleseco-Las Palmas. Las Palmas-Pinar de
  Tamadaba. Pinar de Tamadaba-Las Pal-
  mas. Las Palmas-Firgas-Las Palmas. Las
  Palmas-Moya. Moya-Las Palmas. Las Pal-
  mas-Gáldar. Gáldar-Las Palmas. Las Palmas-
  Agaete. Agaete-Las Palmas. Las Palmas-San
  Nicolás de Tolentino. San Nicolás de Tolentino-
  Las Palmas.

Carretera del Sur

Las Palmas-Telde y regreso. Las Palmas-
  Aguimes y regreso. Las Palmas-San Barto-
  lomé de Tirajana. San Bartolomé de
  Tirajana-Las Palmas. Cruce de Sardina-San
  Bartolomé. San Bartolomé-Cruce de Sardina.
  Las Palmas-Maspalomas y regreso. Las
  Palmas-Arguineguin. Arguineguin-Las Pal-
  mas. Las Palmas-Puerto Rico. Puerto Rico-
  Las Palmas. Las Palmas-Mogán. Mogán-Las
  Palmas.

Carretera del Centro

Salidas desde la calle General Franco, esquina
  San Nicolás

Las Palmas-Tafira-Santa Brígida y regreso. Las
  Palmas-San Mateo. San Mateo-Las Palmas.
  Las Palmas-Tejeda. Tejeda-Las Palmas.

Líneas marítimas
Lignes maritimes
Maritime lines
Schiffsverbindungen
Bätturer mellan öarna

Compañías españolas
Compagnies espagnoles
Spanish companies
Spanische Gesellschaften
Spamska Foretag

AUCONA. Muelle Santa Catalina.

COMPAÑÍA TRASATLÁNTICA ESPAÑOLA, S. A.
Agente: Aucona.
COMPAÑÍA NAVIERA PINILLOS. Agente. Ibérica Canaria, S. A. Plaza del Ingeniero Manuel Becerra (Edificio Puerto).
IBARRA Y CIA., S. A. Agente: Juan Bordes Claverie. Triana, 118.
NAVIERA AZNAR, S. A. Albareda, 32.
ANTONIO ARMAS CURBELO. General Vives, 69.
NAVIERA MIÑO, S. A. Agente: Manuel Toledo y Cía. Plaza del Ingeniero Manuel Becerra. (Edificio Puerto.)
NAVIERA DE CANARIAS. Agente: Mavacasa. Edificio Frisu.

Compañías extranjeras
Compagnies étrangeres
Foreign companies
Auslandische gesellschaften
Utlandska Foretag

Inglesas. Anglaises
Englis. Englische. Engelska

BRITISH INDIA STEAM NAVIGATION CO. LTD. ONE. Aldgate. Londres.
ELLERMANN & BUCKNALL STEAMSHIP CO. 12-20. Camomile Street. Londres.
P. & O. ORIENT STEAM NAVIGATION CO. 2 Gravel Lane. Londres.
ELDER DEMPSTER LINES. India Building. Water Street. Londres.
SHAW SAVIL & ALBION CO. 88 Leadenhall Street. Londes. Agente: Miller y Cía. Muelle Santa Catalina.
THE UNION CASTLE MAIL STEAMSHIP CO. 2 St. Mary Axe. Londres.
BLUE STAR LINE LTD. 3 Lower Regent Street. Londres.
THE CUNARD STEAMSHIP CO. LTD. Canute Road. Southampton.
LAMPORT & HOLT LINE LTD. Royal Liver Building. Liverpool.
PALM LINE LTD. Salisbury Square. Londres.
GLEN LINE LTD. 16 St. Helens Place. Londres.
BIBBY LINE. Water Street. Liverpool.
BLUE FUNNEL LINE. India Building. Liverpool. Agente: Elder Dempster (C. I.) Ltd. Muelle Santa Catalina.

Francesas. Françaises. French
Französische. Franska

COMPAGNIE DE NAVIGATION PAQUET. 90 Boulevard des Dames. Marsella.
NOUVELLE COMPAGNIE DE PAQUEBOTS. 70-72 rue de la République. Marsella. Agente: Miller y Cía. Muelle Santa Catalina.

Otras compañías
D'autres compagnies
Other companies
Andere gesellschaften
Andra bolag

EGON OLDENDORFF. Ecke Beckergrube. Lubeck.
HAMBURG-SUDAMERIKANISCHE DAMPESCHIFFAHRTS. Ost. Weststr, 59. Hamburgo. Agente: Ahles & Rahn. Juan Rejón, 87.
NORDDEUTSCHES LLOYD. Gustav Deetjen Allée 2/6. Bremen.
HAMBURG - AMERIKA LINIE. Ballingdammstr. 25. Hamburgo.
OLDENBURG-PORTUGIESISCHE DAMPFSCHIFFS RHEDEREI. Kajenstr. 10. Hamburgo. Agente: A. Paukner. Albareda, 50.
HUGO STINNES TRASOZEAN SHIFFARHRT. Postfach 1768. Mulheim-Ruhe. Agente: Corporación Ibero-Africana, S. A. José María Durán, 6.
SVENSKA AMERIKA LINIEN. P. 01 Box 2185. Gothenburg. (Suecia).
SWEDISH AMERICAN LINE. 636 Fifth Avenue. Nueva York. Agente: Hamilton y Cía. Juan Rejón, 99, 2.º.
BLUE STAR LINE CALMEDIA. Leadenhall Street. Londres.
DANSK-FRANSKE DAMPSKIBSSELSKAB. 17 Frederiksgade. Copenhague. Agente: ECOPESA. Explanada Tomás Quevedo.
EMPRESA INSULANA DE NAVEGAÇAO. Rue Aurea, 181. Lisboa.
ACHILE LAURO. Via Cristóforo Colombo, 45. Nápoles.
FORENEDE DAMPSIBS-SELSKAB. Sankt Annae Plads, 3. Copenhague. Agente: Guillermo Olsen & Co. Albareda, 48.
JUGOSLAVENSKA LINISJKA PLOVIDBA. Rijeka.
JADRANSKA LINISJKA PLOVIDBA. Rijeka. Agente: Sogemar, José María Durán, 6.
EPIROTIKI LINES. 2. Bubulinas Street. Pireo (Grecia). Agente: Mavacasa. Edificio Frisú.
KELLER SHIPPINGS, S. A. Holbeinstrasse 68. Basilea (Suiza).
CONCORDIA LINE. 90 Broad Street. Nueva York. Agente: Corporación Ibero-Africana. José María Durán, 6.
FINLAND SYDAMERIKA LIJNEN. P. O. Box 6 030. Helsinki.
HOLLAND-AFRIKA LIJN. P. O. Box 922. Amsterdam.
ITALIA S. P. A. Piazza de Ferrari, 1. Génova.
LLOYD TRIESTINO SPA DI NAV. Piazza dell'Unitá di Italia. Trieste.
VAN NIEVELT GOUDRIAAN & COPO Box 825. Rotterdam.
LION FERRY A/B. Färjstationen. Halmstad (Suecia).

REDERI S/B TRANSATLANTIC. Farck 403. Gothenburg (Suecia). Agente: Miller y Cía. Muelle Santa Catalina.

COMPAGNIE MARITIME BELGE, S. A. 61 Rempart Sainte Catherine. Amberes.

FARRELL LINES INC. One Whitehall Street. Nueva York.

JOHNSON LINE. Stureplan, 3 Estocolmo.

HOLLAND-AMERICA LINE. P. O. Box 486. Rotterdam. Agente: Elder Dempster (C.I.) Ltd. Muelle Santa Catalina.

COMPANHIA COLONIAL DE NAVEGAÇAO. Rua de San Juliao, 63. Lisboa.

COMPANHIA NACIONAL DE NAVEGAÇAO. Rua de Comercio, 85. Lisboa. Agente: Camilo Martinón. Pedro del Castillo, 2.

Existen enlaces marítimos interinsulares y con la Península.

Información sobre el estado de las carreteras
Renseignement sur l'état des routes
Information on road conditions
Auskunft über den Zustand der Landstrassen
Upplysningar om landsvägarnas framkomlighet

TELERRUTA MOP (cinta grabada). Telfs. (91) 254 28 00 y (91) 254 50 05. Estado de carreteras y puertos por temporales de nieves y lluvias, y posibles desvíos por obras. Servicio permanente.

Información general del pavimento, distancias y caminos más convenientes para un determinado itinerario, llamar al teléfono (91) 253 16 00, solicitando el Servicio «no grabado» de Telerruta. Horario: invierno, de 8,30 a 22 horas; verano, de 8,30 a 20,30 horas.

Líneas aéreas-Lignes aériennes
Air lines-Luftfahrtgesellschaften
Flygbolag

Las Palmas de Gran Canaria

Vuelos internacionales, con la Península, a Europa, África y América.

AEROPUERTO.

IBERIA. León y Castillo, 5. Oficinas en el Aeropuerto.

AIR FRANCE. León y Castillo, 253.

CALENDONIAN-BUA. Alfredo L. Jones, 33.

KLM. León y Castillo, 246.

LUFTHANSA. Sagasta, 90.

ROYAL AIR MAROC. Presidente Alvear, 25.

AIR AFRIQUE. León y Castillo, 253 (Air France).

SABENA. León y Castillo, 322.

SOUTH AFRICAN AIRWAYS. León y Castillo, 409.

TAP. León y Castillo, i hörnet med Avenida Mesa y López.

AIR SPAIN. Mas de Gaminde, 36.

SAS. Albareda, 48.

SPANTAX. León y Castillo, 248, 2.°.

AIR INDIA. Montevideo, 4.-Oficina de ventas.

ALITALIA. Avda. de Escaleritas, 126, 7.°.

SWISS AIR. Generalagen: Elder Dempster. Mlle. Santa Catalina.

Lanzarote

IBERIA. Avda. Generalísimo Franco, 10. Arrecife. Servicios diarios a Las Palmas, Tenerife y Fuerteventura. Varios vuelos semanales a la Península.

Fuerteventura

IBERIA. General Linares, 15. Puerto Rosario. Servicios diarios a Las Palmas, Tenerife y Lanzarote.

Aero-taxis. Aéro-taxis
Air-taxis. Air-taxis
Air-taxis

Las Palmas de Gran Canaria

HELICSA. Edificio Este. Junta de Obras del Puerto.

5. FIESTAS Y ESPECTÁCULOS
FÊTES ET SPECTACLES
FESTIVITIES AND SPECTACLES
FESTE UND SCHAUSPIELE
LOKALA FESTLIGHETER OCH NÖJEN

5.1. CLUB Y SOCIEDADES DEPORTIVAS
CLUBS ET SOCIÉTÉS SPORTIVES
CLUBS AND SPORTING SOCIETIES
KLUBS UND SPORTVEREINE
KLUBBAR OCH FORENINGAR

Las Palmas

CLUB DE GOLF. Bandama (Tafira).

CLUB DE INVESTIGACIONES SUBACUÁTICAS. Pío XII, 67.

CLUB DE MOTONÁUTICA. Muelle Sta. Catalina.

CLUB NATACIÓN METROPOLE. Paseo Alonso Quesada, s/n.

CLUB NÁUTICO. León y Castillo, s/n.

CLUB DE TENIS. Parque Doramas.

CLUB DE TIRO DE PICHÓN. El Rincón.

TIRO NACIONAL DE ESPAÑA. Polígono de la Isleta.

CLUB DE VELA LATINA. Padre Cueto, 2.

CLUB VICTORIA. Paseo de las Canteras, 3.
CLUB DE AJEDREZ. Terrero, 1.
SOCIEDAD DE CAZADORES. Torres, 11.
U. D. LAS PALMAS. Pío XII, 29.
AEROCLUB. El Berriel, km 46. Carretera del Sur.
REAL AUTOMÓVIL DE G.C. Galo Ponte, 8, 1.º.
TOURING CLUB. Hermanos García de la Torre, 2.
ESTADIO INSULAR.
ESTADIO MARTÍN FREIRE. San José.
ESTADIO ANTONIO ROJAS. Rehoyas.
ESTADIO LÓPEZ SOCAS. Escaleritas.
NUEVO CAMPO ESPAÑA. Calle Zaragoza.
CANCHA DE BALONCESTO DE LA OBRA SINDICAL DE EDUCACIÓN Y DESCANSO.
CANCHA DE BALONCESTO DEL COLEGIO DEL CORAZÓN DE MARÍA. Ciudad Jardín.
CANCHA DE BALONCESTO (INFANTILES) DE GUINIGUADA, GUANARTEME Y JARDÍN DE LA INFANCIA.
CANCHAS DE BALONCESTO Y BALONMANO DEL GRUPO ESCOLAR SANTA CATALINA. Tomás Miller, 65.
CANCHA DE BALONCESTO DEL CLUB METROPOLE.
GIMNASIO DE LAS PALMAS. José María Durán, 6.
BOLERA DEL HOTEL SANTA CATALINA.
BOLERA «EL RAYO». Ripoche, 4.
GOLF. Campo de Bandama, del Club de Golf de Las Palmas. Situado a 12 kilómetros de Las Palmas, por la carretera del Centro. A 450 metros de altura, 18 hoyos. Recorrido, 5 679 metros «Greens» de hierba especial. Par-72. El Club de Golf tiene posada y restaurante.
CAMPO DE MASPALOMAS. Situado junto al oasis de Maspalomas, 9 hoyos. Recorrido, 3 236 metros. Par-72. «Greens» de hierba Bermuda especial. Restaurante y hotel próximos.
TENIS. Pistas de cemento del Club de Tenis. Parque Doramas. Los hoteles «Maspalomas Oasis», en Maspalomas; «Costa Canaria», en San Agustín, y «Santa Brígida», en Monte Corello, tienen pistas para sus clientes, al igual que los apartamentos «Los Caracoles», en San Agustín. Pista en la playa de la Garita (Telde).
GOLF MINIATURA. Parque Santa Calina. Las Laderas (San Agustín).
HIPISMO. Picaderos en carretera de Marzagán. Urbanización La Estrella. Playa de Maspalomas y Club de Golf de Bandama.
JUDO. En el Gimnasio. Las Palmas. José María Durán, 6.
MONTAÑISMO. En el macizo montañoso de Tejeda.
DEPORTES NÁUTICOS. Pueden practicarse en toda época el esquí acuático, el balandrismo, la pesca submarina, etc.

LUCHA CANARIA. Deporte antiquísimo y tradicional, basado en la habilidad y fortaleza de los luchadores para derribar al adversario. Suelen celebrarse por equipos compuestos de 12 hombres, que van eliminándose dos a dos. Las luchas se celebran en el Estadio López Socas, de Las Palmas, y en los pueblos de Telde, Ingenio, Agüimes, Guía y Gáldar.
BOXEO. Las veladas se celebran en el Estadio Insular y el Campo España.
PELEAS DE GALLOS. La temporada va desde el mes de febrero al de mayo. Se celebran los días festivos por la mañana, en la gallera instalada provisionalmente en el Frontón Dania.

Lanzarote

CASINO CLUB NÁUTICO. Blas Cabrera Felipe, s/n.
CLUB MERCANTIL. Avda. de la Mancomunidad.
COMPLEJO POLIDEPORTIVO «AVENDAÑO PORRUA».

Fuerteventura

CASINO EL PORVENIR. Barranquillo.
CLUB DEPORTIVO HERBANIA. Juan Domínguez Peña, s/n.
CLUB DEPORTIVO UNIÓN PUERTO. General Linares, s/n.
SOCIEDAD DEPORTIVA TENICOSQUEY. R. González Negrín, s/n.
ESTADIO POLIDEPORTIVO MUNICIPAL. Los Pozos.
OASIS CLUB. Calle S. Alonso. Cancha de tenis, baloncesto y balónvolea.
SOCIEDAD DEPORTIVA TENISCOSQUEY. Cancha de tenis y piscina.

Piscinas
Piscines
Swimming pools
Schwimmbader
Simmbassanger

Las Palmas

PISCINA JULIO NAVARRO. Parque Doramas (50 metros).
PISCINA CLUB NATACIÓN METROPOLE. León y Castillo, 336 (50 metros).
PISCINA REAL CLUB NÁUTICO. León y Castillo (50 metros).
PISCINA DE LA ISLETA. Jardín de la Infancia (25 metros).
PISCINA HOTEL METROPOL (25 metros).
PISCINA DE LOS APARTAMENTOS VILLA EDEN. Paseo de la Cornisa.
PISCINA HOTEL SANTA CATALINA.

PISCINA DEL HOTEL REINA ISABEL. Avda. Canteras.
PISCINA DEL HOTEL LAS PALMAS PALACE. (Casa del Marino).

5.2. CAZA Y PESCA
CHASSE ET PÊCHE
HUNTING AND FISHING
JAGD UND FISCHFANG
JAKT OCH FISKE

CAZA. La caza puede practicarse en las tres islas de la provincia.
PESCA. La pesca es marítima y puede practicarse en las islas en sus diferentes variantes. Pesca submarina, particularmente en Lanzarote y Fuerteventura y en los islotes aledaños a éstas.

CHASSE. La chasse peut se pratiquer dans les trois îles de la province.
PÊCHE. Le pêche est maritime et peut se pratiquer dans ses îles, dans ses diverses variantes. Pêche sous-marine, particulièrement à Lanzarote et Fuerteventura, et les îlots voisins.

HUNTING. One can hunt on the three islands of the province.
FISHING. Fishing here is all maritime and can be practiced in many different ways on the islands. Submarine fishing, especially on Lanzarote and Fuerteventura and on the small islands nearby.

JAGD. Die Jagd kan auf aen drei Inseln der Provinz ausgeübt werden.
FISCHFANG. Wird auf verschiedene Arten im Meer betrieben von allen Inseln aus. Unterwasserfischfang vor allem in Lanzarote und Fuerteventura und den nahgelegenen kleinen Inseln.

JAKT. Man kan jaga på tre av öarna.
FISKE. Man kan idka havsfiske på alla öarna och med stora variationer. Undervattensfiske kan man idka särskillt på öarna Lanzarote och Fuerteventura, även på klippöarna.

5.3. ESPECTÁCULOS-SPECTACLES
SHOWS-SCHAUSPIELE-NOJEN

Salas de fiestas-Cabarets
Night Clubs-Tanzlokale
Nattklubbar

Las Palmas

ALTAVISTA. Ciudad Jardín Alta.
CANARIAS NIGHT CLUB. Pelayo, 16.
NUMBER ONE. Secretario Artiles, 87.
LA DOLCE VITA. José M.ª Durán, 30.
COPACABANA. Bernardo de la Torre, 100.

FLAMINGO. F. González Díaz, 1.
PINITO DEL ORO. Portugal, 30.
EL HUECO. Paseo de Madrid, 1.
SIETE MARES (SEVEN SEAS). Nicolás Estévanez, 29.
HALF NOTE JAZZ SHOW. Nicolás Estévanez, 57.
EL BOMBÍN (THE BOWLER HAT). Grau Bassas, 39.
TAMADABA. El Veril. Playa del Inglés.
ALOHA. Blasco Ibáñez, 57.
ACAPULCO. Ferreras, 12.
ALHAMBRA CLUB. Ripoche, 16.
BONGÓ. Ripoche, 22.
LA CACATÚA. Alfredo L. Jones, 23.
LA CARIOCA. Joaquín Costa, 63.
CINTRA CLUB. Joaquín Costa, 48.
CLUB 69. Pedro del Castillo, 10.
EL COFRE. Sagasta, 40.
LA GRUTA. La Naval, 7.
MAHEY. Los Martínez de Escobar, 39.
EL TRÉBOL. Dr. Miguel Rosa, 37.
EL VOLCÁN. Sargento Llagas, 3.
LA BELLA ÉPOCA. Nicolás Estévanez, 67.
LA LUNA. Frente al aeropuerto de Las Palmas.
LUTECE. Néstor de la Torre, 36.
PACHA CLUB. Los Martínez de Escobar, 68.
SAXO JAZZ. Sagasta, 3.
LA VENUS. José María Durán, 30.
TAM TAM. Pi y Margall, 12.
WHISKY CLUB. Bernardo de la Torre, 87.
YACHT CLUB. Joaquín Costa, 37.
TUSSET STREET. Montevideo, 2.
JEROME CLUB 2 000. Concepción Arenal, 16.
GOYA. Bernardo de la Torre, 86.
CIRO. General Primo de Rivera.
JACARANDA. Ripoche, 4.
PIGALLE. El Veril. Playa del Inglés.
LAS OLAS. Apart. «Las Olas». Playa del Inglés.
KYOTO. Apart. «Jardín del Atlántico». Playa del Inglés.
MONTE DEL MORO. Playa de San Agustín.
BEACH CLUB. Playa de San Agustín.

Tablaos flamencos
Spectacles flamencos
Flamenco shows
Flamencovorstellungen
Flamencodanser

Las Palmas

FLAMENCO'S. Torres Quevedo, 17.
LAS BRUJAS. Edificio Mercurio. Playa del Inglés.

Cinematógrafos
Cinémas
Movies
Kinos
Biografer

Las Palmas

ASTORIA. F. Guanarteme, 44.
AVELLANEDA. Herrería, 11.
AVENIDA. General Franco, 51.
BAHÍA. Secretario Artiles, 22.
CAPITOL. Tomás Morales, 23.
CARVAJAL. Carvajal, 60.
CUYÁS. Viera y Clavijo, 11.
REX. Eusebio Navarro, 69.
RIALTO. Presidente Alvear, 3.
ROYAL. León y Castillo, 40.
SOL. Gerona, 2.
VEGUETA. Padre José de Sosa, 22.

Teatros
Théâtres
Theathers
Theater
Teatrar

Las Palmas

TEATRO PÉREZ GALDÓS. Lentini, 1.

6. TURISMO

6.1. EXCURSIONES A LOS ALREDEDORES
EXCURSIONS AUX ENVIRONS
EXCURSIONS ROUN AND ABOUT
AUSFLÜGE IN DIE UMGEBUNG
UTFLYKTER I OMGIVNINGARNA

GRAN CANARIA

TEROR. Estación veraniega del interior, a 11 km de Arucas. Posee extensísimas campiñas, limitada por imponentes macizos montañosos, en donde se asienta en amplio y derramado caserío. La mayor fama de la villa le viene dada por el santuario de la Virgen del Pino.

TEROR. Station estivale de l'arrière-pays. La ville, située à 11 kilomètres d'Arucas, est entourée d'une campagne très étendue, limitée par d'imposants massifs montagneux, où l'exploitation agricole est en plein essor. Teror est surtout célèbre à cause du sanctuaire de la Vierge du Pin.

TEROR. A summer resort in the interior just ó 1/2 miles from Arucas, it has extensive pine woods bounded by impressive mountains and is the selting for a number of scattered settlemen. The fame of the village comes from the fact that it is the site of the Shrine of the Virgen del Pino.

TEROR. Sommerkurort im innern, 11 km von Arucas enifernt. Der Ort besitzt ausgedehnte Anbaugebiete, die durch wuchtige Bergmas-

sive begrenzt werden; die Häuser eligen weit verstreut, Sas Dorf ist durch das Heiligtum der «Virgen del Pino», beruhmt.

TEROR. Sommarort i inlandet, 11 km från Arucas. Stor, spridd bebyggelse, omgiven av vidsträckta fält och imponerande bergmassiv. Orten är mest känd för sin kyrka tillägnad talljungfrun «Virgen del Pino».

ARUCAS. En el centro de una feracísima vega, con el más extenso e importante campo de palmeras del archipiélago. Interesante iglesia parroquial de puro estilo gótico. Junto a la ciudad, el cono volcánico llamado de la Montaña de Arucas, desde cuya cima se contempla amplio y bello panorama, con el Puerto de la Luz y las montañas de la Isleta.

ARUCAS. Située au centre d'une plaine très fertile ou se trouvent les plantations de palmiers les plus importantes de l'archipel. Intéressante église paroissiale de pur style gothique. A côté de la ville se trouve le cône volcanique qui porte le nom de Montagne d'Arucas, du sommel duquel on peut admirer un vaste et beau panorama, le Puerto de la Luz et les montagnes de l'Isleta.

ARUCAS. In the center of an extremely fertile plain with the largest and most important palm grove in the Archipelago. There is an interesting parish church in pura Gothic. Near the city is the volcanic cone known as the Montaña de Arucas from the top of which there is a lovely panorama faking in the Puerto de la Luz and the mountains of the isleta.

ARUCAS. Der Ort liegt inmitten eines äusserst fruchtbaren Anbaugebietes mit dem grössten und bedeutendsten Palmenwald des Archipels. Interessant ist die Plarrkirche in reinem gotischen Stil. Bei der Stadt erhebt sich der Vulkankegel La Montaña de Arucas; von seinem Gipfel aus überblickt man ein weites, schönes Panorama mit dem Puerto de la Luz und den Bergen der Isleta.

ARUCAS. Beläget mitt i en fruktbar floddal, med ögruppens största och viktigaste palmskog. Intressant församlingskyrka i rent gotisk stil. Nära staden finns vulkankäglan Montaña de Arucas, varifrån man har en vidsträckt, vacker utsikt över Puerto de la Luz och bergen på Isleta.

GUÍA. Próspera ciudad del Norte, junto a la Punta de Guanarteme. Interesantes fallas del imaginero canario Luján Pérez en la iglesia parroquial. En la inmediaciones, el Cenobio de Valerón, compuesto por una serie de cuevas cobijadas bajo un formidable alero de lavas.

GUÍA. Ville prospère du nord, proche de la pointe de Guanarteme. Sculptures intéressantes de l'artiste canarien Luján Pérez, dans l'église paroissiale. Non loin de la se trouve le Cenobio de Valerón, composé d'une série de grottes abritées sous un formidable auvent de laves.

GUÍA. A prosperous city to the north next to the Punta de Guanarteme, it offers interesting works by the Canaries sculptor, Luján Pérez, in the parish church. Nearby is the Cenobio de Valerón, a series of caves sheltered by a formidable covering of lava.

GUÍA. Aufstrebende Stadt im Norden bei der Punta de Guanarteme. Interessante Schnitzareien des kanarisschen Bildhauers Luján Pérez in der Pfarrkirche. In unmittelbarer Nähe liegt der «Cenobio de Valerón», der aus einer Reihe von Höhlen besteht, die durch ein riesges Lavadach geschützt werden.

GUÍA. Välmående stad på nordkusten invid Punta de Guanarteme. I församlingskyrkan finns intressanta träsniderier av dem infödde skulptören Luján Pérez. I närheten ligger klostret Valerón som består av en rad grottor, skyddade av ett utskjutande tak av lava.

GÁLDAR. Ciudad de especial interés histórico y arqueológico. Vestigios de la cultura guanche, principalmente en Cueva Pintada, en la que existen pinturas geométricas en diferentes colores.

GÁLDAR. Ville présentant un intérêt historique et archéologique spécial. Vestiges de la culture guanche, principalement dans la grotte Pintada, où il y a des peintures géometriques de diverses couleurs.

GÁLDAR. A city of special historic and archeological interest, there are relics of the Guanche culture, principally in the Cueva Pintada, in which there are geometrical designs in diferent colors.

GÁLDAR. Diese Stadt ist besonders historisch und archäologisch interessant. Funde der Guanchen-Kultur, hauptsächlich in Cueva Pintada; dort wurden geometrische Malereien in verschiedenen Farben gefunden.

GÁLDAR. Intressant ur historisk och arkeologisk synpunkt. Lämningar av guanchekulturen, huvudsakligen i Cueva Pintada där det finns geometriska figurer i olika färger.

AGAETE. Bella ciudad de gran solera marinera, junto al valle de Agaete, largo y zigzagueante cañón plantado de plátanos, cafetos, papayas, aguacates, maíz, etc. Yacimientos arqueológicos de Malpís, declarados Munumento Nacional. En medio de exuberante vegetación, a siete kilómetros, se encuentra el balneario de los Berrazales, con un manantial de aguas ferruginosas.

AGAETE. Belle ville au caractère maritime remarquable près de la vallée d'Agaete, long cañón en zigzag planté de bananiers, de caféiers, de papayers, d'avocatiers, de maïs, etc. Gisements archéologiques de Malpaís, classé monument national. La station thermale des Berrazales (sources ferrugineuses est à 7 kilomètres, au milieu d'une végétation exuberante.

AGAETE. A beautiful city next to the Agaete Valley, a long, sig-zagging canyon planted with banana tress, coffee trees, papayas, alligator pears, corp, etc. The archeological remains at Malpaís have been declared a National Monument. Just over 4 miles away, in a region of exuberant vegetation, is the spa of Berrazales with a spring of ferriferous waters.

AGAETE. Die schöne Stadt liegt beim Valle de Agaete, einem im Zickzack verlaufenden, tief ausgewaschenen Flusstal, wo Bananenstauden, Kaffeesträucher, Papayas, Avocatobirnen, Mais, usw, gedei hen. Archäologische Funde in Malpaís, die unter Denkmalschutz stehen. In einer Entfernung von 7 km und inmitten einer üppigen Vegetation befindet sich der Badeort Los Berrazales mit einer elsen haltigen Quelle.

AGAETE. En vacker stad med sjöfartstraditioner invid den långa, slingrande Agaetedalen. I denna odlas bananer, kaffe, papaya, avocado, majs, etc. Den arkeologiska fyndplatsen i Malpaís har blivit officiellt förklarad historiskt minnesmärke. Sju kilometer från Agaete, inbäddad i frodig grönska, ligger badorten los Berrazales, vars källa ger järnhaltigt vatten.

MOGÁN. Uno de los núcleos de población más importantes del sur de la isla. Bellísimos paisajes de rocas y suelos calcinados, con estrechos barrancos.

MOGÁN. Un des centres les plus peuplés du sud de l'île. Magnifiques paysages de roches calcinées et de ravins étroits.

MOGÁN. One of the most important population centers in the southern part of the island, it presents extremely beautiful scenes of calcinated rocks and earth cut by narrow ravines.

MOGÁN. Eine der wichtigsten Ortschaften im Süden der Insel. Herrliche Landschaften mit Felsen und ausgeglühtem Boden sowie engen Schluchten.

MOGÁN. Ett av öns viktigaste samhällen i söder. Vackert, ökenartat landskap med klippor och smala raviner.

ARGUINEGUÍN. Pequeña población junto a la Punta del Perchel. Litoral óptimo para la pesca de altura, con servicios adecuados para la práctica de este deporte.

ARGUINEGUÍN. Petite localité à côté de la pointe du Perchel. Littoral rêvé pour la pêche en haute mer. Services spéciaux assurés pour la practique de ce sport.

ARGUINEGUÍN. A tiny town near Punta del Perchel. An ideal region for deep-sea fishing, it provides adequate facilities for this sport.

ARGUINEGUÍN. Kleiner Ort bei der Punta del Perchel. Die Küste ist bestens geeignet für den Hochseelischfang und werfügt über die entsprechenden Einrichtungen für diese Sportart.

ARGUINEGUÍN. Ett litet samhälle invid Punta del Perchel. Kusten här är idealisk för djuphavsfiske, med tillgång till all behövlig service.

MASPALOMAS. Playa de 6 000 metros de longitud, prolongación de la anterior y una de las más bellas de la isla. Muy próximo existe un amplio y tupido oasis formado por palmeras y matorrales de marismas, y junto al oasis, una pequeña albufera, en la que se practica la pesca y el remo.

MASPALOMAS. Plage de 6 000 mètres de longuer, prolongement de la précedente et une des plus belles de l'île. Tout à côté, se trouve une grande oasis touffue, formée de palmiers et de plantes de marais. Près de l'oasis, un petit étang où l'on pratique la pêche et le canaloge.

MASPALOMAS. A 3 1/2 mile beach, the extension of the previous one, it is one of the loveliest on the island. Nearby there is a fine «oasis», formed by palms and dune shrubs, next to which is a small lagoon which is used for fishing and rowing.

MASPALOMAS. Der 6 000 m lange Strand ist die Fortselzung des vorhergehenden und einer der schönsten der Insel. Ganz in der Nähe liegt eine grosse, üppige Oase mit Palmen und Gebüsch und nicht weil davon eine kleine Bucht, die für Fischfang und Rudersport sehr geeignet ist.

MASPALOMAS. Plagen som är 6 000 lång, utgör fortsättning på den föregående och är en av öns vackraste. Helt nära ligger en stor oas där palmer och sumpmarksbuskar växer tätt, och invid casen en saltvattensjö där man kan fiska och ro.

INGENIO. Localidad famosa especialmente por sus bordados.

INGENIO. Localité connue surtout à cause de ses broderies.

INGENIO. Particularly famous for its embroidery.

INGENIO. Dieser Ort ist besonders wegen seiner Stickereien berühml.

INGENIO. Berömt speciellt för sina broderier.

SAN BARTOLOMÉ DE TIRAJANA. A 23 kilómetros de Agüimes, después de muchas revueltas de la carretera, aparece San Bartolomé de Tirajana, en la hoya de un cráter inmenso, situado al pie de los macizos centrales. Son las mayores alturas de la isla: Pozo de las Nieves (1 965 m.) y Pechos (1 961 m.), desde donde se contempla el maravilloso paisaje de la Caldera de Tirajana, los valles de Ayacata y Fataga y sus poblados, con la necrópolis guanche de Arteara; son de gran belleza paisajística.

SAN BARTOLOMÉ DE TIRAJANA. En suivant la route, a 23 kilomètres d'Agüimes, après 'de nombreux tournants, voici San Bartolomé de Tirajana, dans le fond d'un inmmense cratère situé au pied des massifs du centre. Ce sont les points culminants de l'île: Pozo de las Nieves (1 965 mètres), et Pechos (1 961 mètres), d'où l'on peut contempler le merveilleux paysage de la Caldera de Tirajana, les vallées et localités de Ayacata et de Fataga, ainsi que la nécropole guanche d'Arteara.

SAN BARTOLMÉ DE TIRAJANA. 14 miles from Agüimes along a winding road is San Bartolomé de Tirajana; it sits in the botton of an immense crater at the food of the central mountain mass. Here are the highest points on the island: Pozo de las Nieves, 6,485 feet, and Pechos, 6,473 feet, from which may be admired the marvellous scenery of the Caldera de Tirajana, the walleys of Ayacata and Fataga and their villages, with the Guanche necropolis of Arteara, all of them of great scenic beauty.

SAN BARTOLOMÉ DE TIRAJANA. 23 km von Agüimes entfernt faucht nach vielen Windungen der Strasse San Bartolomé de Tirajana auf: es liegt in der Mulde eines riesigen Kraters am Fuss der Zentralmassive. Die höchsten Gipfel der Insel sind: Pozo de las Nieves (1 965 m) und Pechos (1 961 m). Von dort aus übersieht man die wundervolle Landschaft, der Caldera de Tirajana. Die Täler Aycata und Fataga und ihre Dörfer mit der Nekropolis der Guanches in Arteara sind ebenfalls landschaftlich reizvoll.

SAN BARTOLOMÉ DE TIRAJANA. 23 km från Agüimes längs en kurvig väg, ligger San Bartolomé de Tirajana i en jättestor krater vid foten av de centrala bergassiven. Här finns öns högsta: Pozo de las Nieves (1965 m) och Pechos (1 961 m); från den senare har man en strålande utskt över Caldera de Tirajana, Ayacala- och Fataga-dalarna med sina små samhällen och guanchernas begravningsplats i Arteara.

TEJEDA. Centro y vértice de la isla, en cuyas proximidades apunta al cielo el majestuoso Roque Nublo, cubierta y recortada piedra de basalto, y aparece la Cruz de Tejeda, en donde se encuentra un Parador Nacional de Turismo. El paisaje —«Tormenta petrificada», en frase de Unamuno—es de gran belleza, entre almendros, huertas y poderosas cimas, como Bentayga, el Fraile, etc., que dominan espléndidas panorámicas.

TEJEDA. Centre de l'ile où se dresse le majestueux Roque Nublo, masse basaltique qui se découpe sur le ciel. Puis on aperçoit la Cruz de Tejeda, où se trouve un parador national du Tourisme. Le paysage —«tempête pétrifiée», suivant l'expression d'Unamuno— est d'une grande beauté. Amandiers vergers, sommets imposants comme ceux du Bentayga, du Fraile, etc., qui dominent des panoramas splendides.

TEJEDA. Center and heart of the island. Nearby the majestic Roque Nublo, a jagged spike of basalt reaches to the sky and the traveller finds the Cruz de Tejeda, location of a National Tourist Inn. The scenery, «a petrified storm» in Unamuno's phrase, is of great beauty with almond grovers, truck gardens and rugged peaks, such as Bentayga, El Fraile, etc., which look out over splendid panoramas.

TEJEDA. Sie ist Mittelpunkt und zugleich Scheitelpunkt der Insel: in ihrer Nähe ragt der majestatische Roque Nublo aus überaigertem und zerklüftetem Basaltstein in den Himmel. Dort erhebt sich auch die Cruz de Tejeda, wo sich ein staatlicher Parador befindet. Die Landschaft —ein «versteinerter Gewittersturm» nach einem Ausspruch Unamuno— ist von grossartiger Schönheit mit Mandelbäumen Obstgärten und gewaltigen Gipfeln, wie der Bentayga, der Fraile, usw., von deren Höhen sich herrliche Rundblicke bieten.

TEJEDA. Beläget i öns mittpunkt, i vars närhet den majestätiska Roque Nublo skarpa basaltsiluett avtecknar sig mot himlen. Här ligger också Cruz de Tejeda, med ett statligt turisthotell. Landskapet —som Unamuno kallade «en förstenad storm»— är underbart vackert med madelträd, odlingar och mäktiga hölder som t.ex. Bentayga och el Fraile, från vilka man har en härlig utsikt.

TELDE. En tierras productoras de excelente fruto. En los alrededores, Tara conserva maravillosas cuevas de los primitivos pobladores de la isla, y Cuatro Puertas, con el monumento más interesante indigena de la isla, de la época paleolítica, la montaña sagrada de los guanchas.

TELDE. Grande production de fruits excellents. Aux environs, à Tara, il y a des grottes merveilleuses qui furent habitées par des peuplades primitives de l'ile et, à Cuatro Puertas, la montagne sacrée des Guanches, se trouve le monument indigène de l'époque paléolithiques le plus intéressant de l'ile.

TELDE. In an excellent fruit-producing region. In the surrounding area are Tara, which preserves the marvellous cavers of the primitive inhabitants, and Cuatro Puertas with the most interesting relic of the original indians, the sacred hill of the Guanches, from the Paleolthic period.

TELDE. Der Ort liegt in einem fruchtbaren Obstanbaugebiet. In der Umgebung findel man in Tara sehenswerte Höhlen der Ureinwohner der Insel und in Cuatro Puertas den heiligen Berg der Guanchas; er stammt aus dem Paläolithikum und ist das interessanteste Zeugnis aus der Vergangenheit.

TELDE. Jorden här är utomordentligt fruktbar. I det närbelägna Tara kan man bese grottor vilka tidigare beboddes av öns urbefolkning, och i Cuatro Puertas den intressantaste sevärdheten från stenålderstid, guanchernas heliga berg.

LANZAROTE

TEGUISE. Antigua capital de la Isla, señorial y silenciosa. Digna de visitarse es la iglesia de San Miguel. En las proximidades podremos visitar el castillo de Guanapay, antigua fortaleza del siglo XIV, reformado por Torriani, arquiteto de Felipe II, y terminado en 1596. Desde su Torre del Homenaje se divisa en días claros Fuerteventura y las islas menores.

TEGUISE. Ancienne capitale de l'ile, seigneuriale et silencieuse. L'église de San Miguel mérite d'être visitée. Aux alentours, nous pourrons visiter le château de Guanapay, ancienne forteresse du XIVème siècle, modifié par Torriani, architecte de Philippe II et acheve en 1596. De son Donjon, on voit les jours clairs, Fuerteventura et les iles mineures.

TEGUISE. Ancient capital of the island. It is lordly and silent. The church of San Miguel deserves a visit, Nearby, we can visit the castle of Guanapay an ancient fortress of the XIV century, reformed by Torriani, Filip Il's architect, and finished in 1596. From its Tower of Homage, Fuerteventura and the smaller islands can be seen on a clear day.

TEGUISE. Ehemalige Hauptstadt der insel, vornehm. und ruhig. Besuchenswert ist die Michaelskirche. In der Nähe ist das Schloss Guanapay zu besichtigen, eine alte Festung aus dem XIV. Jahrhundert, durch Torriani, den Architekten Philipp II, renoviert und 1596 fertiggestellt. Vom Ehrenturm (Torre del Homenaje) sieht man an klaren Tagen Fuerteventura und die kleineren Inseln.

TEGUISE. Öns forna huvudstad, lugn och förnäm. San Miguel kyrkan är värd ett besök. I närheten kan vi besöka fästningen Guanapay, uppförd på 1300-talet och ombyggd av Filip II:s hovarkitekt Torriani. Arbetet slutfördes år 1596. Från fästningens huvudtorn kan man i klart väder se Fuerteventura och de mindre öarna.

HARÍA. Situada en un valle fértil con sus casas entre las palmeras, da la sensación de un oasis en el desierto.

HARÍA. Située sur une fertile vallée, avec ses blanches maisons parmi les palmiers, elle donne l'impression d'une oasis dans le désert.

HARÍA. Located in a fertile valley with its white houses amid dove cotes, giving the sensation of an aosis in the desert.

HARÍA. In einem fruchtbaren Tal gelegen, mit seinen weissen Häusern zwischen den Palmen gleicht es einer Oase in der Wüste.

HARÍA. Med sina vita hus bland palmer, belägna i en fruktbar dal, liknar samhället en ökenoas.

BATERÍA DEL RÍO. Extraordinario mirador sobre las islas menores, situado en la abrupta costa del Norte.

BATERÍA DEL RÍO. Belvédère vraiement extraordinaire sur les îles mineures, situé sur l'escarpée côte du Nord.

BATERÍA DEL RÍO. A fantastic look-out post over the smaller isles, located on the rugged Northern coast.

BATERÍA DEL RÍO. Hervorragender Aussichtspunkt über die kleineren Inseln, die an der nördlichen Steilküste liegen.

BATERÍA DEL RÍO. Från denna plats på den branta nordkusten har man en fin utsikt över de mindre öarna.

JAMEO DEL AGUA. Cueva subterránea de formación volcánica, prolongación de la Cueva de los Verdes. Su suelo lo constituye un lago.

JAMEO DEL AGUA. Caverne souterraine de formation volcanique, prolongation de la Cueva de los Verdes. Un lac couvre son sol.

JAMEO DEL AGUA. An underground cave of volcanic formation; an extension of the Cueva de los Verdes. Its floor is formed by a lake.

JAMEO DEL AGUA. Unterirdische Höhle vulkanischen Ursprungs, Verlängerung der oben erwähnten Grotte (Cueva de los Verdes). Ein See dehnt sich auf dem Grund der Höhle aus.

JAMEO DEL AGUA. Denna underjordiska grotta av vulkaniskt ursprung utgör fortsättning på Cueva de los Verdes. Dess «golv» bildas av en sjö.

CUEVA DE LOS VERDES. Curiosa gruta de seis kilómetros de longitud, por donde en otro tiempo discurrió la lava volcánica. La isla fue muy castigada por la piratería de los siglos XV y XVI; su población usó la cueva como baluarte natural, saliendo siempre victoriosa de los asedios.

CUEVA DE LOS VERDES. Curieuse grotte de 6 km de longueur, parcourue autrefois par la lave volcanique. L'île fut très châtiée par la piraterie des XVème et XVIème siècles, et sa population employa la caverne comme un bastion de la nature et en sortit toujours victorieuse.

CUEVA DE LOS VERDES. A strange cave 6 km, long which time ago the volcanic lava used to flow through. The island was greatly punished by pirates during the XV and XVI centuries and its townsfolk used the cave as a natural defense, and always proved victorious in seiges.

CUEVA DE LOS VERDES. Eigenartige sechs Kilometer lange Grotte, durch die früher der Lavastrom floss. Die Insel litt sehr unter den Seeräubern im XV. und XVI. Jahrhundert. Daher benützten die Inselbewohner die Grotte als natürliches Bollwerk, das ihnen bei Belagerungen den Sieg sicherstellte.

CUEVA DE LOS VERDES. Genom denna märkliga, sex kilometer långa grotta flöt i tiden den vulkaniska lavan. Under 1400- och 1500-talen, då ön var föremål för piraternas ständiga anfall, använde befolkningen denna grotta som naturlig bastion och utstod på så sätt belägringarna.

ARRIETA. En las proximidades se encuentra la playa de La Garita.

ARRIETA. On trouve dans son voisinage la plage de la Garita.

ARRIETA. Clase by is the beach of La Garita.

ARRIETA. In der Nähe befindet sich der Strand von La Garita.

ARRIETA. I närheten ligger plagen La Garita.

LA GERIA. Es una muestra de la incesante lucha del isleño con la tierra para convertir en campos fértiles unas zonas inhóspitas. Empleando un curioso sistema de agricultura en «macetas», consistente en hoyos profundos cavados en la tierra y protegidos por muros de piedra de lava con que se cubren los cultivos.

LA GERIA. C'est un exemple de l'incessante lutte de l'île avec la terre pour transformer en champs fertiles des zones inhospitalières. Ils emploient un curieux système d'agriculture en «pots», qui consiste à creuser des trous profonds dans la terre, protégés par des murs en pierre de lave; celle-ci recouvre les cultures.

LA GERIA. This is a sample of the islander's incessant struggle with the land to convert inhospitable zones into fertile lands, Using a curious agricultural system called «macetas» they make deep hollows in the land, and protec them by lava stone walls, with which the crops are covered.

LA GERIA. Ein Beispiel für den endlosen Kampf der Inselbewohner mit der Erde um unwirliche Gegenden in fruchtbare Pelder zu verwandeln. Man bedient sich dabei eines eigenartigen landwirtschaftlichen Systems (der sog. macetas): tiele Gräben werden angelegt, wobei eine Schutzmauer aus Lavagestein die Feldfrüchte umgibt.

LA GERIA. Ett bevis på öbornas ständiga kamp mot jorden för att förvandla ogästvänliga områden till bördig odlingsmark med hjälp av ett säreget slags jordbruk i «krukor», bestående av djupa hal som grävts i marken och skyddats med murar av lavasten.

UGA. Pueblo de aspecto africano, con casitas cuadradas rodeadas de palmeras que pone una nota de color en la aridez del paisaje.

UGA. Village d'aspect africain, avec de petites maisons entourées de palmiers qui met une note coloriste dans l'ardité du paysage.

UGA. An African like village, with square huts surrounded by palm trees, which gives a note of colour in the arid landscape.

UGA. Das Dorf mil seinen viereckigen, von Palmen umgebenen, Häusern ein Farbfleck in der dürren Landschaft — macht einen afrikanischen Eindruck.

UGA. Liknar ett afrikanskt samhälle med sina fyrkantiga hus omgivna av palmer som ger färg åt det karga landskapet.

YAIZA. En sus inmediaciones se encuentra el Janubio, lago circular junto a la costa.

YAIZA. Dans son voisinage se trouve le Janubio, lac circulaire près de la côte.

YAIZA. Nearby is the Janubio, a circular lake next to the coast.

YAIZA. In unmittelbarer Nähe befindet sich der kreisförmige Janubio See, unweit der Küste.

YAIZA. I närheten, vid kusten, ligger den cirkelrunda sjön Janubio.

MONTAÑA DEL FUEGO. La ascensión hasta la cima puede realizarse en camello hasta el refugio-mirador, desde donde se domina toda una imponente zona de cráteres y conos volcánicos y el enorme mar de lava, de formas caprichosas y de tonos multicolores.

MONTAÑA DEL FUEGO. L'ascension au sommet peut se faire à dos de chameau, jusqu'au réfuge-mirador (réfuge-belvédère), d'où l'on domine toute une imposante zone de cratères et de cônes volcaniques, et l'énorme mer de lave aux formes capricieuses et aux tonalités multicolores.

MONTAÑA DEL FUEGO. One can go up to the summit by camel, which takes tourists to the look-out shelter, from where a very important zone of craters and volcanic cones and the enormous sea of lava can be contemplated, with its fancy shapes and multi-colour tones.

MONTAÑA DEL FUEGO. Der Aufstieg zum Gipfel kann bis zum Schutzturm auf Kamelen zurückgelegt werden. Von dort überblickt man eine eindrucksvolle Kraterlandschaft mit Vulkangipfeln und ein riesiges Lavameer mit den eigenartigsten Formen und den verschiedensten Farbtönungen.

MONTAÑA DEL FUEGO. Med kamel kan man ta sig upp till toppen. Härifrån ser man ut över ett område av imponerande vulkakäglor och kratrar och det vidsträckta lavahavet, som antar skiftande former och färger.

ISLOTE DE HILARIO. Aquí se registran casi a flor de tierra temperaturas de 400°. Es tradicional efectuar el experimento de la quema de aulagas, introduciéndolas en un hoyo hecho en el suelo, o de freír o asar cualquier alimento, utilizando esa extraordinaria cocina natural que es el suelo de la montaña. Después, el paisaje se va haciendo menos hostil y se atraviesa una zona de tabaco y de tomate; pasamos por Mancha Blanca, donde podemos contemplar la ermita de Nuestra Señora de los Volcanes, el Peñón del Indiano y la Cueva de los Naturalistas.

ISLOTE DE HILARIO. La température atteint ici, à fleur de terre, 400° C. C'est dans la tradition d'effectuer l'experience de brûler les genêts, en les introduisant dans un trou fait dans le sol, frire ou rôtir n'importe quel aliment, en se servant de cette extraordinaire cuisine naturelle qu'est le sol de la montagne.

Après, le paysage se fait moins hostile et on traverse une zone de tabac et de tomates, on passe par Mancha Blanca, où nous pouvons contempler l'ermitage de Nuestra Señora de los Volcanes (Notre Dame des Volcans), el Peñón del Indiano et la Cueva de los Naturalistas.

ISLOTE DE HILARIO. Here temperatures of 400° have been recorded. It is traditional to make the experiment of burning the scorpion-broom, putting it in a hollow dug in the ground, or frying or roasting some foodstuff, using that extraordinary natural cooker, namely the mountain ground.

Later the landscape becomes less hostile and a tobacco and tomato zone is crossed. We can pass Mancha Blanca, where the Shrine of Our Lady of the Volcanoes can be seen, the Rock of the Indiano, and the Cave of the Naturalists.

ISLOTE DE HILARIO. Fast auf der Erdoberfläche werden Temperaturen von 400° verzeichnet. Das Verbrennen der Ginster, die dabei in ein in den Boden gegrabenen Loch gesteckt werden, gehört schon zu den traditionellen Experimenten, oder das Kochen oder Braten irgendwelcher Nahrungsmittel auf diesem ausgezeichneten Ofen, den die Bergerde bietet.

Danach wird die Landschaft weniger unwirtlich, man durchquert Tabak- und Tomatenpflanzungen und kommt durch Mancha Blanca, wo man die Kapelle Nuestra Señora de los Volcanes, die Indianerfelskuppe (el Peñón del Indiano) und die Naturforscherhöhle (Cueva de los Naturalistas) besichtigen kann.

ISLOTE DE HILARIO. Här har man uppmätt temperaturer på 400° strax under jordytan. Det är brukligt att göra provet att bränna gultörne i en grop i marken, och steka eller grilla någon mat på denna ovanliga naturliga spis som utgörs av berggrunden.

Sedan blir landskapet mindre ogästvänligt, och vi kör genom tobaks- och tomatodlingar, vi passerar Mancha Blanca där vi beser kapellet tillägnad vulkanjungrun «Nuestra Señora de los Volcanes», Peñón del Indiano och Cueva de los Naturalistas.

SAN BARTOLOMÉ. Típico pueblo, famoso por sus danzas folklóricas.

SAN BARTOLOMÉ. Typique village fameux pour ses damses folkloriques.

SAN BARTOLOMÉ. A typical village, famous for its folklore dances.

SAN BARTOLOMÉ. Typisches Dorf, wegen seiner volkslümlichen Tänze berühmt.

SAN BARTOLOMÉ. En typisk Lanzaroteby, berömd för sina folkdanser.

FUERTEVENTURA

COTILLO. Castillo de planta circular construido en el siglo XVII, que sirvió en tiempos para combatir las expediciones berberiscas en las costas del norte de la Isla.

COTILLO. Châteaux de plan circulaire, construit au XVIIème siècle, et qui servit en son temps pour combattre les expéditions mauresques contre les côtes du Nord de l'Île.

COTILLO. A circular castle built in the XVII century, which time ago was used fo fend olf the Berber expeditions on the Northern coasts of the Island.

COTILLO. Kreisförmig angelegtes Schloss aus dem XVII. Jahrhundert, von dem aus früher die Berbereinfälle an der Nordküste der Insel bekämpfte.

COTILLO. Fästning uppförd på cirkelformad grund på 1600-talet. Begagnades i tiden för att avvärja berbernas anfall mot öns nordkust.

LA AMPUYENTA. Magnífica iglesia amurallada dedicada a San Pedro de Alcántara.

LA AMPUYENTA. Magnifique église munie de murailles, consacrée à San Pedro de Alcántara.

LA AMPUYENTA. A magnificent walled church, dedicated to Saint Peter of Alcántara.

LA AMPUYENTA. Herrliche, dem Hl. Petrus von Alcántara geweihte Festungskirche.

LA AMPUYENTA. Ståtlig kyrka, omgiven av murar, tillägnad San Pedro de Alcántara.

BETANCURIA. Reúne esta villa el conjunto monumental más importante de la isla, con su antigua catedral donde se guardan objetos de culto de gran belleza y antigüedad, así como el pendón de la conquista de la isla. Subsiste parte del convento del que fue guardián San Diego de Alcalá y la cueva donde éste se retiraba en oración. La iglesia tiene el característico estilo medieval.

BETANCURIA. Cette ville réunit l'ensemble monumental le plus importan de l'île, avec son ancienne cathédrale, où l'on garde des objets de culte d'une grande beauté et antiquité, comme l'étendart de la conquète de l'Ile. Y existe encore une partie du Couvent dont fut gardien San Diego de Alcalá, et la caverne oú celui-ci se retirait pour prier. Lestyle médiéval est caractéristique del'église.

BETANCURIA. This Ilage has the most important monumental collection on the island, with its anciennt cathedral, where very beautiful and ancient objects of worship are kept, and ealso the Standard of the island's conquest. Part of the Convent that Saint Diego de Alcalá was guardian of, still remains, and the Cave where he retired to for prayer. The church has the characteristic Medieval style.

BETANCURIA. In dieser Stadt befinden sich die meisten Baudenkmäler der Insel: die alte Kathedrale, die wunderschöne und antike Messgegenstände auf bewahrt, sowie die Eroberungsstandarte der Insel: ein Teil des Klosters, dessen Vorsteher der Hl. Diego von Alcalá war, und die Höhle, in der er sich im Gebet zurückzog. Die Kirche weist den charakteristischen mittelalterlichen Baustil auf.

BETANCURIA. Här finns öns förnämsta samling historiska byggnader, bland dem katedralen där man bevarat vackra gamla kultföremål samt fanan som bars vid öns erövring. En del av klostret där San Diego de Alcalá var föreståndare står kvar, likson den grotta till vilken han drog sig tillbaka för att bedja. Kyrkan är uppförd i karakteristisk medeltidsstil.

VEGA DE RÍO PALMA. En el valle se encuentra el santuario de la Virgen de la Peña, patrona de la isla. Es una imagen pequeña de alabastro y posiblemente la más antigua del archipiélago.

VEGA DE RÍO PALMA. Dans la vallée on trouve le Sanctuaire de la Virgen de la Peña, patronne de l'île. C'est une petite statue d'albâtre et, peut-ètre la plus ancienne de l'archipel.

VEGA DE RÍO PALMA. In the valley is the Shrine of Our Lady of the Rock, the Island's Patron Saint. Il is a small alabaster statue and possibly the oldest ine in the Archipelago.

VEGA DE RÍO PALMA. Im Tal befindet sich das Heiligtum der «Virgen de la Peña». Es ist ein kleines Alabasterbildnis, möglicherweise das älteste der Inselgruppe.

VEGA DE RÍO PALMA. I dalen ligger kapellet tillägnat klippjungfrun «Virgen de la Peña», öns skyddshelgon. Hon är avbildad i en alabasterstatyett, möjligen den äldsta som finns på ögruppen.

PAJARA. Interesante el pórtico de la iglesia, en cuya piedra se encuentran tallados geométricos motivos aztecas.

PAJARA. Intéressant portique de l'église sur la pierre duquel on trouve taillés de nombreux motifs géometriques aztèques.

PAJARA. The church portico is of interest. In the stone, are engravings of geometric Aztec motifs.

PAJARA. Sehenswertes Kirchenportal mit geometrischen Steinreliefs aus der Geschichte der Azteken.

PAJARA. Kyrkans portik är intressant; i dess stenar är inhuggna geometriska aztekmotiv.

TUINEJE. Pueblo que sufrió numerosos ataques de piratas ingleses y berberiscos y del que se conservan algunos resquicios.

TUINEJE. Village qui supporta de nombreuses attaques des pirates anglais et mauresques et dont on conserve quelques restes.

TUINEJE. This village suffered numerous attacks from British pirates and Berbers, and some glimpses of these still remain.

TUINEJE. Das Dorf litt unter zahlreichen Piratenüberfällen der Engländer und Berber, wovon noch Spuren erhalten sind.

TUINEJE. Samhället bär spår av de talrika överfall det utsatts för av engelska och nordafrikanska sjörövare.

CALETA DE FUSTES. En las proximidades se encuentra un castillo de planta circular que data del siglo XVII. La playa en forma de herradura guarda en las profundidades de sus aguas un santuario submarino con una imagen de la Virgen de la Peña.

CALETA DE FUSTES. On trouve dans ses alentours un château de plan circulaire qui date du XVIIème siècle. La plage, en forme de fer à cheval, garde dans la profondeur de ses eaux, un sanctuaire sour-marin avec une statuette de la Virgen de la Peña (La Vierge du Rocher).

CALETA DE FUSTES. Nearby is a circular castle which dates back to the XVII century. The horseshoe shape beach has an underwater shrine with a statue of the Virgin of the Rock, in its deep waters.

CALETA DE FUSTES. In der Nähe befindet sich ein kreisförmig angelegles Schloss aus dem XVII. Jahrhundert. Der hufeisenförmige Strand umschliesst ein in der Tiefe gelegenes Heiligtum mit dem Bildnis der «Virgen de la Peña».

CALETA DE FUSTES. I närheten finns en fästning från 1600-talet, uppförd på cirkelformad grund. Utanför den hästskoformade plagen finns ett undervattenskapell med en statyett av klippjungfrun «Virgen de la Peña».

6.2. ALTITUDES Y DISTANCIAS KILOMÉTRICAS DESDE LAS PALMAS A:
ALTITUDES ET DISTANCES KILOMÉTRIQUES DEPUIS LAS PALMAS A:
ALTITUDES AND DISTANCES IN KILOMETERS FROM LAS PALAMAS TO:
HÖHENLAGEN UND ENTFERNUNGEN IN KILOMETERN VON LAS PALMAS NACH:
HÖJDER OCH KILOMETRISKA STRÄCKOR FRAN LAS PALMAS TILL:

	Distancia Distance Entfernung Avstand	Altitud Altitude Höhenlage Höjd
Agaete	49	43
Agüimes	29	259
Arguineguín	64	10
Artenara	46	1 219
Arucas	17	240
Cruz de Tejeda (Parador Nacional)	35	1 451
Fataga	65	525
Firgas	25	466
Fontanales	42	525
Galdar	40	123
Gando (Aeropuerto de)	26	8
Guía de Gran Canaria	37	180
Ingenio	27	264
Maspalomas (Playa de)	59	8
Mogán	104	253
Moya	30	490
Monte Coello	10	427
San Bartolomé de Tirajana	58	895
Santa Brígida	14	520
Santa Lucía de Tirajana	51	680
San Mateo	22	950
San Nicolás	84	90
Tafira	8	375
Tamadaba (Pinar de)	51	1 460
Tamaraceite	7	185
Tejeda	44	1 050
Telde	14	116
Teror	21	543
Valleseco	27	950
Valsequillo	24	558

DISTANCIAS KILOMÉTRICAS DESDE ARRECIFE A:
DISTANCES KILOMETRIQUES DEPUIS ARRECIFE A:
DISTANCES IN KILOMETERS FROM ARRECIFE TO:
ENTFERNUNGEN IN KILOMETERN VON ARRECIFE NACH:
KILOMETRISKA AVSTAND FRAN ARRECIFE TILL:

Haría	28
Femes	25
San Bartolomé	25
Teguisa	11
Tias	10
Tinajo	15
Yaiza	23
Las Coloradas	25
La Geria	17
Timanfaya	28
Islote de Hilaria	33
Jameos del Agua	27
Cuevas de los Verdes	25
La Betaria	34
Isla Graciosa	40
Isla Alegranza	59
Orzola	33

DISTANCIAS KILOMÉTRICAS DESDE PUERTO ROSARIO A:
DISTANCES KILOMÉTRIQUES DEPUIS PUERTO ROSARIO A:
DISTANCES IN KILOMETERS FROM PUERTO ROSARIO TO:
ENTFERNUNGEN IN KILOMETERN VON PUERTO ROSARIO NACH:
KILOMETRISKA AVSTAND FRAN PUERTO ROSARIO TILL:

Tetir	8
La Oliva	28
Corralejo	44
Casillas del Ángel	12
La Antigua	22
Betancuria	28

ÍNDICE

PUBLICACIONES EVEREST
SOBRE LAS ISLAS CANARIAS

● **GUÍAS ARTÍSTICO-TURÍSTICAS**

— GRAN CANARIA-LANZAROTE-FUERTEVENTURA, por
  M. González Sosa.
  Ediciones en español, francés, inglés y alemán.
— TENERIFE-LA PALMA-GOMERA-HIERRO, por Enrique
  García Ramos.
  Ediciones en español, francés, inglés y alemán.
— COSTAS DE ESPAÑA, por J. A. García Barquero.
  Edición en español.
— Guía Informativa de Gran Canaria, Lanzarote y Fuerte-
  ventura (español, francés, inglés, alemán y sueco).

● **COLECCIÓN IBÉRICA**

— FUERTEVENTURA EN COLOR (español, francés, inglés y
  aleman).
— GOMERA-HIERRO EN COLOR (español, francés, inglés y
  alemán).
— GRAN CANARIA EN COLOR (español, francés, inglés y
  alemán).
— LANZAROTE EN COLOR (español, francés, inglés y ale-
  mán).
— LA PALMA EN COLOR (español, francés, inglés y alemán).
— TENERIFE EN COLOR (español. francés, inglés y alemán).

- **COLECCIÓN HISPÁNICA**

— FUERTEVENTURA
  (Ediciones en español, francés, inglés y alemán).
— GOMERA-HIERRO
  (Ediciones en español, francés, inglés y alemán).

- **CLUB EVEREST**

— ESPAÑA TURÍSTICA

- **MAPAS TURÍSTICOS DE ESPAÑA**

— MAPA CARTOGRÁFICO DE LAS ISLAS CANARIAS.
— MAPA TURÍSTICO DE LANZAROTE Y PLANO DE ARRE-
  CIFE.
— GUÍA-CALLEJERO DE LAS PALMAS DE GRAN CANARIA.
— PLANO-CALLEJERO DE LAS PALMAS DE GRAN
  CANARIA.